It's How You Play The Game: Olympic Sports in York

Van Wilson

Published by York Archaeological Trust 2012
47 Aldwark, York YO1 7BX
www.yorkarchaeology.co.uk

Designed and typeset by Lesley Collett,
York Archaeological Trust Publications Dept.

Cover design by Lesley Collett

Printed by B&B Press, Rotherham

ISBN No. 978-1-874454-58-8

*Front cover: Olympic silver medal crew 1980 (Allan Whitwell); Anita Lonsbrough at
Cambridge Road Baths January 1963 (Kirklees Image Archive and Huddersfield Daily Examiner);
Olympic medals.*
*Back cover: Stan Wild, gymnast and Olympic torchbearer, on rings at Olympic Games 1968
(Stan Wild); Clive Warley, table-tennis player and Olympic torchbearer 2012 (Clive Warley)*

CONTENTS

FOREWORD

by ANITA LONSBROUGH, MBE

Gold medal winning swimmer Anita Lonsbrough was born in York in 1941. She won gold for the 200 metre breaststroke in the 1960 Olympics, and gold medals in the 1958 and 1962 British Empire and Commonwealth Games. Anita was the first BBC woman Sports Personality of the Year in 1962 and the first woman to carry the British flag at the Olympics, in Tokyo, in 1964.

Anita Lonsbrough at Cambridge Road Baths, January 1963
(Kirklees Image Archive and Huddersfield Daily Examiner)

I was born in York. My father was a Regimental Sergeant Major in the Coldstream Guards and was posted to India. My mother and I followed him out there where we stayed for around nine months. When we first returned to the UK we were

v

based in Magull [Merseyside]. *My father was then posted to Penny Pot Lane just outside Harrogate. He retired from the army in the summer of 1955 and took a job in Huddersfield.*

Both my parents were keen on sport. My father played many sports whilst my mother was a keen cyclist and swimmer and used to swim in the Ouse one mile race. I enjoyed training and racing. My father had always instilled into me, if anything was worth doing it was worth doing well. It was not all about winning but doing the best I could.

Anita Lonsbrough with her many swimming trophies, December 1962
(Kirklees Image Archive and Huddersfield Daily Examiner)

ACKNOWLEDGEMENTS

We would like to thank the following for their generous support in helping fund this project: Friends of York Archaeological Trust, Sheldon Memorial Trust, Patricia and Donald Shepherd Charitable Trust, the Yorkshire Architectural and York Archaeological Society, Robert Kiln Charitable Trust and Yorkshire Philosophical Society.

I am grateful to those who have given me information about particular sports and have allowed me to copy photographs –

Keith Baker, Alan Johnson and Keith Wood of the York Railway Institute Pistol and Rifle Club, Amanda Booth of Kirklees Image Archive, Kate Cartwright, MBE, for photos of her brother Anthony and father Paddy Power, Joel Kerry, local studies librarian, Heather Kirby for photos and information about boxers Fred and Harry Kildin, Stephen Lewis, Chief Feature Writer and Stuart Martel, Sports Editor of the York Press, Peter Monahan of York Railway Institute, Martin Pinder, Noel Porter, Ann Robinson, Jim Spriggs, Ian Tempest, David Thurlow and Alex Wilson from National Union of Track Statisticians for their athletics information, Janet Pigott for photos of Joss Watson and York Oral History Society.

My grateful thanks are due to Mike Race, Chairman of York Oral History Society, for the use of his interviews with Reg Butler and Alf Patrick, for help with transport to interviews, for spending many hours copying photographs for the project and for information about his uncle, Olympian Harold Porter.

From York Archaeological Trust I would like to thank the Chief Executive, John Walker, and Sarah Maltby, Director of Attractions, for their continuing support, Mike Andrews for scanning photographs and Lesley Collett for her design and layout of the book. Most of all I am indebted to Christine Kyriacou, Archivist and Editor, for managing the project, as well as excellent fundraising and painstaking proof-reading.

My thanks go to Anita Lonsbrough for writing the foreword of this book, and to the following for sharing their stories (and photos) about their particular sport –

Harry Atkins, Derek Bellerby, Peter Bibby, Terry Boyes, John Bunyan, Peter Burbidge, Karen Burdass and Pauline Clarkson, Reg Butler, Maureen Chevens, Mike and Angela Craggs, Mags Felter, Frank Richard Fowler, Norman Fowler, Paul Hobman, Malcolm Huntington, Denis Jackson, Bryn Jones, John Linfoot, Jamie MacLeod, Brooke Midgeley, Guy Mitchell, Cathy Mitton, Anne Morrice, Alf Patrick, David Poole, Anthony Power, Tom Quinn, Michael Saville, Brian Snelson, Alan Sparks, Les Tomkinson, Angela Tooby-Smith, Charlie Twissell, Clive Warley, Allan Whitwell, Stan Wild, Walter Wilkinson, Keith Wood, Dennis Woodcock.

INTRODUCTION

'Sport is human life in microcosm'
Howard Cosell

2012 is a significant year for sport with London hosting the Olympic Games for the third time, the only city to do so. Hopes are pinned on several British squads and the Olympics promise to be stylish, splendid, dramatic and thrilling.

When one thinks of York, the subject of sport does not immediately spring to mind. The best facilities tend to be in the bigger cities, London, Bristol and Nottingham, and in the north, Sheffield and Bradford. The sports for which York is best known, such as cricket, rugby, bowls and horse-racing, are not Olympic sports. Harry Gration, BBC sports commentator and TV presenter, who wrote the foreword for my last book (on Clifton), has covered much about these in his book 'Yorkshire Sporting Heroes'.

But York has had its share of sportsmen and women who have excelled in Olympic sports, whether locally, nationally or internationally. There are few, if any, publications about these minority sports and I wanted to concentrate on York-born sportsmen and women, or those who have lived in the city for a substantial amount of time.

There have been York Olympians, from gold medallists, swimmer Anita Lonsbrough and hockey player Richard Dodds, silver medallist rower Allan Whitwell, table tennis Paralympian and bronze medallist Cathy Mitton, to competitors such as wrestler Arthur Thompson, gymnast Stan Wild, athletes Wally Beavers, Stanley Engelhart and Harold Porter, swimmers Pauline Musgrove, Peter Kendrew, Amanda Radnage, fencer Anthony Power, pentathlon athlete George Norman, as well as Olympic tennis umpire Malcolm Huntington. There are others working towards the Olympics like Tom Quinn, canoeist, rower Tom Ransley and runner Richard Buck. There have also been many who did not reach Olympic heights but who have still proved their worth in their particular sport.

Whilst we have made every effort to find Olympians and other successful athletes in the city, and advertising of the project has been widespread, it is possible that names have been missed. Those whose stories appear in these pages are representative of all who have been successful in some way in Olympic sports in York.

Van Wilson
May 2012

— Chapter 1 —
ARCHERY

Historically, the longbow used in archery was a weapon of war as opposed to a tool of sport. Archery began as an Olympic sport in Paris in 1900, but as there was no international consensus for its governance, it was banished in the 1920s and did not return until 1972. York Archers, founded in 1833, is one of the oldest clubs still in existence in the UK.

Early archery meeting c1850s. (Les Tomkinson)

The idea of first instituting a Grand National Archery Society originated at a meeting of archers at the Black Swan in York in May 1844, convened by William Gray, secretary to the Thirsk Bowmen. Rules were drawn up and about 70 archers attended the event in August, from as far afield as Sherwood Forest, Glasgow and Kingston. £125 was contributed for prizes, with the chief prize being 50 guineas. Further meetings were held in 1846 and 1852. By the beginning of the 20th century the city had two archery clubs, the White Rose Archers and the York Archers.

Les Tomkinson is a member of the latter, though he spent a few years with another club, Ebor Archers, initially.

LES TOMKINSON

The first Grand Archery Meeting was held in York on the 1st of August 1844. That was a fabulous event, it wasn't just the shooting, there were balls, a perform-ance at the theatre, grand dinners, all very regal and spectacular.

There are three types of bows. When they started there were longbows. A piece of wood from Victo-rian times, they were made

York Theatre Royal poster - entertainment for the First Grand National Archery Society 1844.

(Les Tomkinson)

in laminated wood, something like hickory and degame. One wood that's good in compression, one that's good in tension, you put them together and you get a spring. Then you bend it, you get quite a lot of force and you can shoot arrows with it.

The yew longbow, sometimes it was British yew, but usually Spanish yew. You still have people who will make yew long-bows, but they cost a minimum of about £300. Most British yew takes a long time to grow. It tends to be full of pins and knots.

Archery began to decline in the 17th century. By about 1685, it was more or less dead as a weapon of war. It wasn't picked up

2

until the late 18th century, the gentry started to get involved and they took it up as a sport. They'd play what they called rovers. You take a bow and a couple of arrows, walk out into a field and pick a mark. The guy who gets the shot nearest the mark picks the next shot. There was lots of pomp and ceremony and marching bands, a real social occasion. And then there was that little fella, Napoleon, the gentry got a bit sidetracked. They had to go and deal with the serious matters of war. It wasn't until after 1815 that they started to pick it up again. So if you had money, a few hours to spare, it was a good thing to do. A group of archers called the Archers of the Finsbury Mark in London set up marks in particular parts of the field, and target archery grew from that. People would practise for an hour or so at the local butts and there were plenty of them at York. The one that I'm most convinced existed was in Walmgate between the Bar and the Retreat, just a piece of open ground. They'd pile earth up and put marks on them.

Admission ticket for First Grand National Archery Society meeting, August 1844 (Les Tomkinson)

Ladies Day, Royal Toxophilite Society, July 1893 (Les Tomkinson)

1833 they'd be shooting with longbows, they shot on the Knave-
smire which is hilarious when you think of the health and
safety we've got now.

Les and his wife Elaine came back to York in 1974.

We'd been living out at Tadcaster. There was a thing on at
'Sport for All' at Rowntree Park on Sunday so we went down
and met Ebor Archers who were doing a 'havagosa', very short
distance, very simple fibre glass bows and wooden arrows. You
got half a dozen arrows and had a shot at the target. So we
were taught to shoot. Then we both became quite good at it and
stayed, got equipment and started going to tournaments. 1975
was the first real tournament year. And we had a bit of success
there. You had either longbows or re-curve bows which are the
modern Olympic weapon. In '78, Elaine became county cham-
pion, she won it three years consecutively. Then in 1980 she

4

broke the British record for the Hereford Rout. And that record's never been broken, it still stands in Yorkshire. It became our life for a long time. And then we started a family. You can't do archery when you've got small children so we retired.

But later, their two children decided to take up the sport too.

You need a bow, arrows, a tab which is a leather finger guard for your hand so you don't tear the skin off your fingers, and a thing called a bracer which fits on the arm that you hold the bow with, to stop the string whacking your arms and causing bruising. Nowadays arrows are a lot more complicated than the wooden shafts that the Victorians had. They are aluminium tubes, sometimes wrapped in carbon fibre. And they can be £40 each. If you're shooting tournaments, you need a dozen. So it

Archery Demonstration, Lord Mayor's Gala, Knavesmire 1976. Les Tomkinson is in centre. (Les Tomkinson)

5

can be about £500 for arrows and you wouldn't get much change out of £1000 for a good bow.

The compound bows are the ones with wheels. You get a lot of mechanical advantage so they're much more powerful than a normal bow. When you draw the bow, you mustn't draw it higher than level with the ground. It goes a fair long way so it will land way behind the target, because it's an arrow that's not properly guided.

Elaine Tomkinson,
Yorkshire champion
June 1979
(Les Tomkinson)

The things that are likely to break are the limbs. Because they are a sandwich of fibre glass, carbon fibre, maple, just glued together with very special glue. Of course they flex each time you shoot the bow, so they get quite a lot of umpty over the years. But they're pretty resilient. Buying a bow is a bit like buying a suit. What will suit one person won't suit another. There'll be a range of handles, the middle bit which we call the riser, and the arrow rest. You have to be careful about how heavy the bow is when you pull it. The worse thing you can be is over-bowed. You can kill a good archer by making his bow too heavy.

Ebor Archers were at the Civil Service Club on Boroughbridge Road. It's a big ground. There was always space to put a target up. We'd shoot a round or a few dozen of an evening at different distances, and then on a Sunday we'd shoot a round which is set distances. Fantastic if you're husband and wife and you can do something like that. It makes you better at your sport. They call it the Jack and Jill. We were northern counties Jack and Jill champions for two or three years, in the early '80s.

If you shoot a York round, the round shot in York in 1844, which is six dozen at 100 yards, four dozen at 80 yards and two dozen at 60 yards, it can be a real slog to shoot that number of arrows. Nowadays it's quite different. They have eliminators and head to heads, much more complex.

We run at least six courses a year. Elaine is the beginners' officer for York Archers. I'm the records officer so if you shoot scores, I log them. We coach the first batch, we don't throw them in at the deep end and see if they drown, we'll keep an eye on them. It's a long process making an archer. You've got to practise to go on a tournament, be physically and mentally prepared. The way most people lose is by worrying about what other people are doing.

Target number 1, last end at 60 yards East Yorkshire Championships Burton Constable 1981.
Les Tomkinson has arm over target. (Les Tomkinson)

The judges have very little to do at a tournament. If people
have equipment failure, if something falls off or a string breaks
they'll stop the shoot and you can have 15 minutes to repair it.
The judges are in charge of safety. If you hear somebody shout,
'Fast', short for 'Stand fast', you stop shooting and you put
your hand in the air. But you don't get many accidents.

We're very lucky in York Archers because that is set up as an
archery range and nothing else happens there. It's on Malton
Road, near the Hopgrove. We have just short of 100 members.
It's about 60/40 men to women. If you go back to Victorian
times, there were no ladies at first.

If you practise enough, you'll become quite good. If you're at a tournament every week, your name starts to become known. The scores will give you a classification. Archer, third class archer, second class archer, first class archer, bowman, master bowman and grand master bowman, when you're floating about two feet off the floor. There aren't that many of those. Tracy McGowan who shoots with us, shot in the Commonwealth Games [2010], she's a grand master. Mark Franklin who's her partner, he is grand master. Both shoot compound bows, and it's not legal for Olympic competition. They have sights, telescopes and levels. When we were shooting, Elaine made master bowman quite early on. The score that she made is still grand master bowman. If you want to be selected, you have to write to the county secretary and say these are the scores. And you'll be selected from a panel. I made the county team a couple of times. Elaine was remarkable for the time because she was leading the rest of the ladies by a long way. To get to Olympic standard, you'll probably have a British record under your belt.

The person you've got to beat on that field is you. You only ever shoot against yourself, because you are your own worst opponent. You've got to be calm and remain calm. I remember watching Elaine on the day that she broke the British record. Of all the romantic places in the world it was Bingley. I remember thinking she had a sort of aura. The maximum score is 1296. She shot 1182, that was the record. People who win really don't care about anybody else, they're in their own little bubble. It takes tenacity, patience. Got to be able to take whatever the opposition throws at you. The best archers, some of the Korean women, they're within a tenth of a second each time they shoot. And they are so accurate. They can out-shoot archers with compound bows, with a re-curve bow. I can sit and watch archers shoot. For anybody else it's like watching paint dry. It's really annoying watching the Olympics because you can't pick

9

faults. They're all so good. It really is their life. There's a stage of your career, when you go from being somebody off the street into becoming a novice archer, to archer, then to whatever you want. You do get sponsorship now. We were all strictly amateur. You do get people who'll get bows given or arrows or whatever. That's really good because it allows people to flourish in an environment where they're not worried about having to pay for all the stuff.

It's expensive in terms of money and time. But isn't everything that's worth doing? In the history of archery, you read about medieval tournaments, there's no doubt archery was part of everybody's life from the age of seven. They'd give a boy a bow stave, when he was seven he'd get a bow, just the stave not string. He'd stand and hold it. After about a year, they'd let him string it, give him an arrow and he'd learn to draw it. And by the time he was 12, he was already developing arthritis. The bows were fantastically heavy, upwards of 150 pounds. Modern re-curve bows, you'd expect somebody drawing 48 to 50 pounds. Sebastian Flute, gold medallist at the 1990 Olympics, he was shooting 500 arrows a day and holding 52 pounds on his fingers. That's a lot of weight. That's a lot of commitment.

It's just dedication. You have to give it everything, because if you don't, you'll never make it. Elaine and I were lucky because we travelled together, we shared everything, we experienced the same things.

Sarah Beamish, one-time member of York Archers, shot for Yorkshire in 2007 to 2009, and has shot for Great Britain since 2009. She won silver in the Stoke Mandeville Para Event in 2011, and team silver in the Para World Championships. She is in line to compete at the 2012 Paralympics.

— *Chapter 2* —
ATHLETICS

Athletics is the oldest sport in the world and has the most categories at the Olympic Games. There are 47 events divided into four strands – track, which has 24 events (12 events for men, 12 for women), 16 field events (8 each for women and men), two combined events (decathlon for men, heptathlon for women), and five road events (men's and women's marathons, men's and women's 20 km race walks and men's 50 km race walk). In 2012 there will be 2000 athletes competing in these events.

York Harriers torch carriers. Boys in white left to right – Peter Sankey, John England (obscured), David Poole, Kenneth Johnson, Robert Paxton (David Poole)

YORK HARRIERS

York Harriers and Athletic Club was founded at a meeting at the Queen's Head, Fossgate in September 1898, to 'foster and encourage athletes, mainly running and walking'. The club was affiliated to the Northern Counties Athletics Association. In 1902, the most notable member was J Meek who created a record of running over 11 miles in an hour.

Enthusiasm tailed off, and then the First World War intervened. A meeting to revive the Harriers was held at the Bay Horse, Blossom Street in January 1919.

According to a 1937 membership card, the club's headquarters were at the Racing Stables in Dringhouses and Sir Francis Terry, Director of Terry's Factory, was the president. A women's section was added to the club in 1931.

As part of the celebrations during the York Festival in 1954, the Harriers made a torch-lit circuit of the city walls two nights a week for three weeks. At the Fire Brigade Social Room in Clifford Street, the 30 runners changed into a white kit with blue shoulder sash, and moved to Clifford's Tower to assemble. As there were not enough men still in the Harriers, they engaged the help of a group of boys from the York Boys' Club, including David Poole, who recalls,

> *The torches consisted of a stout wooden baton about two feet in length, topped with a metal holder containing paraffin and a fabric wick. As dusk fell, the runners formed into two organised teams, led by Harold (Bob) Clark who had international cross country honours, and Peter Littlewood, the Harriers' captain. A lot of people turned out to see us. The final run on 4th July started at 11.25pm so that the teams would arrive at the Mansion House for 11.45pm, from where they led the official procession* [consisting of the Lord Mayor and Corporation, the cast of the Mystery Plays and others who had taken part in the festival] *to the south door of the Minster for the service.*

The torch weighed heavy after half a mile, and although it was possible to switch from hand to hand, a flagging arm brought the danger of singed locks, especially if there was a stiff breeze. An extinguished flame could be rekindled from a neighbour and the mildly acrid smell was tolerable. The worst problem was the multitude of steps on the Walls. A shout from the leader of 'Four up' or 'Two down' was usually adequate warning.

The Harriers Club numbered many successful athletes amongst its members, including three Olympians. The club closed in the 1960s and a separate club, Knavesmire Harriers, was set up in the 1980s.

WALLY BEAVERS

Walter James 'Wally' Beavers was born in York in 1903 and became a member of the York Harriers in his teens. He won nine Northern Counties titles for one mile, three miles and four miles. He was selected for the Olympics in 1928 in Amsterdam. He finished ninth in the 1000 metre event and ran against the 'Flying Finn', Paavo Nurmi, who won gold.

In 1929, Wally won the City of Hull trophy for best performance at the annual championships, for the four mile event. His career continued into the 1930s and he won the three mile (now 5000 metres) AAA championship at Stamford Bridge (Chelsea football ground) in London in 1932. The AAA (Amateur Athletic Association)

Wally Beavers and Harold Porter 1924
(Mike Race)

13

York Harriers AC 2 mile team with trainers Knavesmire 1924. Athletes L to R
- Harold Porter, Wally Beavers, R W Cammdige, W Richardson. (Noel Porter)

had been set up in 1880 as a national governing body for the sport. Wally had also competed in the Northern Counties Athletics Association three mile event on Leeds University track. W. Illingworth tells the story, "All the outstanding distance runners in the North were there, but Beavers was soon nearly 100 yards behind them and was subject to some barracking from the crowd. What many spectators did not know was that Beavers was running according to a strict schedule set by his coach Jimmy Dawson. Dawson shouted 'Tha's all reight, Walter', as he came past him. Two and a half laps from the finish, Jimmy called out, 'Nah then Walt, tha can go', and with a phenomenal burst of speed, Beavers overhauled his famous rivals. His time of 14 mins 38.4 seconds was not beaten until 1949". Later a rule was brought in to ban any members of the public from the arena. Wally's highest achievement was to win gold in the three mile contest at the 1934 British Empire Games (which became in 1970 the British Commonwealth Games).

Wally Beavers was definitely a character. David Thurlow of NUTS, the National Union of Track Statisticians, was told the story that on one occasion Wally was offered money to lose a two mile race, but he had backed himself with the bookies to win. He won the race and to avoid the complications which might ensue, he had a taxi with the engine running outside to take him to the station. In Paris for an international, Wally and another of the British team decided to celebrate. Having had a little too much to drink, they were unfortunately arrested. They taught the gendarme (guarding them in the cells overnight) how to play pontoon. They let him win and won their freedom.

Wally died in 1965 but is still remembered in the athletics fraternity, and is considered to be one of York's greatest athletes.

STANLEY ENGELHART

Stanley Engelhart, born in Selby in 1910, was another successful member of the York Harriers. At the 1930 Empire Games he won silver in the 4 x 110 yards, and gold at the 220 yards event, completing in 21.8 seconds. This ensured his selection for the 1932 Olympic Games in Los Angeles. Unfortunately he suffered a pulled muscle which meant

Stanley Engelhart winning the 220 yards against France at Stamford Bridge, 1930.

early elimination in the 200 metres event, but he was a member of the British relay team which finished sixth.

HAROLD PORTER

Harold Porter joined York Harriers in 1919 when he was only 16, and was a member of the strong cross country team well known in the north. He was Yorkshire champion at 880 yards, one mile and three miles. Harold was selected for the Olympic Games, and ran in 1924 in Paris, the year of Eric Liddell and Harold Abrahams, made famous in the film *'Chariots of Fire'.*

It was said at the time that the British squad was 'the most powerful athletic force ever to leave these shores'.

Harold Porter at Olympic Games, Paris 1924

(*Noel Porter*)

Harold Porter's identity card for the 1924 Olympics (Noel Porter)

Olympic Games programme, Paris 1924 (Noel Porter)

The Yorkshire Gazette of 28th June 1924 explained that Harold 'has brought a great honour to the city by being selected as representative of Great Britain in the 3000 metres flat race in the Olympic Games. He gave a very creditable performance in the AAA championships on Saturday when he finished third in the mile race, only four fifths of a second behind the winner'. When he got to Paris, Porter was thrilled to be representing his country and to be received by the Prince of Wales.

The semi-final of the 3000 metres race took place on 11th July, the same day that Eric Liddell won the 400 metres. First place went to Paavo Nurmi, second and third places also went to Finland and Porter finished fourth, the first British man home from the four man team. Britain overall finished second and qualified for the final on 13th July. The Yorkshire Evening Press reported that Porter 'ran splendidly for the British team'. The heat on both days was intense, at 88 degrees Fahrenheit, with great humidity. British competitors were supplied with light caps to shield them from the sun but two athletes were still too unwell to travel home with the rest of the squad at the end of the Games.

York Harriers York AC 2 mile team, early 1920s. Back row – Wally Beavers, W Richardson. Front row – Harold Porter, R W Cammidge. (Mike Race)

In the final on the 13th July, Porter came tenth, (and fourth out of the British competitors) and the British team won silver medals. The Yorkshire Gazette reported that Porter 'ran well … and the fair name of York was worthily upheld in the Olympic Games', so his own city was definitely proud of him.

There is an anomaly about this race. Members of his family who researched Porter's achievements contacted the official Olympic

Association, and were told that Harold Porter won a silver medal. The official Olympic website, which lists all medallists for every Olympic Games in history, also states that Porter received silver. But other sites and publications explain that only the first three Britons were awarded a medal and Porter, because he was fourth, returned home empty-handed. Alex Wilson of NUTS states that, 'There is no mention in the 1924 Olympic report of medals being awarded to non-scorers in the 3000 metre team race. I believe that only the actual scorers [ie. the first three] in the final would have received silver medals'. It seems therefore that the official information is incorrect and Harold did not receive a silver medal.

What made it doubly hard for him was that George Webber, the third British man in the race, did not even finish the semi-final heat on 11th July, (so would have been less tired than the other men) yet was allowed to run in the final, and finished only seconds ahead of Harold. The medals won by Bert MacDonald, one of the trio who did get silver, were sold in 2010 at Sotheby's for £3000.

After the Games, Harold Porter was selected to run in an international race on 16th July in Stamford Bridge, London, representing

Great Britain against the USA. It was a four mile relay race, and Porter took the first leg. There were 25,000 spectators. In August, he won three championships in one week; the four miles Yorkshire championship at Gisburn near Keighley, the Yorkshire mile championship and the half mile championship at Castleford. He celebrated his 21st birthday in the same month and stopped running two years later.

Olympic medals sold at Sotheby's

(Ian Tempest)

When Harold retired in 1967, he was given a presentation to mark 50 years of service at the North Eastern Electricity Board. His workmates were astonished to hear that he had once been an Olympic runner and had run in international meetings against France, Scotland, Wales, Ireland and the USA. His boss described him as 'a quiet unassuming man ... not everyone was aware of his success on the running track'. During his time as an athlete, he won many prizes including grand-father clocks, ornaments, silver bowls and a trunk full of towels and sheets. But it is unlikely that he won an Olympic medal. He died in 1970 aged 76.

RICHARD BUCK

Richard Buck, a British sprinter specialising in 400 metres, was born in 1986 and attended Lady Lumley's School in Pickering. He joined the City of York Athletics Club (formerly Nestlé Athletics Club) at the age of 14, with his grandfather as sprint coach. He won bronze at the 400 metre event at the 2004 Commonwealth Youth Games in Australia. In 2007 he represented Great Britain at both the World Student Games and was part of the relay squad at the World Athletics Championships in Osaka. He was selected for the 2008 Olympics but unfortunately a virus affected his training and he could not take part. He won international medals throughout 2009 to 2011 and in 2012 won silver in the 400 metres relay in the world indoor championships in Istanbul.

After appearing on television and mentioning the withdrawal of his funding from UK Athletics, Richard was overjoyed to receive a £10,000 donation from an anonymous 90 year old man. He was also given a car by BMW. This has meant he could leave the job he had to take in a supermarket and concentrate on training.

ANGELA TOOBY-SMITH

Angela Tooby-Smith was born in Herefordshire but now lives in York and teaches at St Peter's School.

She won the Welsh Cross Country Championships four times in 1984–1987, finishing eighth at the World Cross Country Championships in 1984. She was the 10,000 metres bronze medallist at the 1986 Commonwealth Games. After winning silver at the 1988 World Cross Country championships, she ran in the women's 10,000 metres race at the 1988 Games.

Angela Tooby (in front) and twin sister Susan warming up for World Cross Country Championships 1988 (Angela Tooby-Smith)

LES RICHARDS

There have not been many York field athletes of renown, but York's Les Richards is ranked second in the country for indoor shot put, with a distance of 16.99 metres. His return to the international ranks, after representing Great Britain at under 17 and under 23 level, came less than a year after he had undergone surgery for a back injury. He began as a discus thrower but injury led him to change to the shot put.

His York Athletics Club coach Paul Wilson also hopes that Les will qualify for the 2012 Olympics. "He's passionate about his sport and dedicated to it".

JOHN SHERWOOD

John Sherwood was born in 1945 in Selby but now lives in Sheffield, where he has retired from 40 years of teaching. He represented Great Britain in the 1968 Olympics in Mexico, winning a bronze medal in the 400 metre hurdles. At the same Olympics, his wife Sheila won silver for the long jump.

In 1965, Walter Wilkinson and John Sherwood were joint winners of the Pepsi Cola award, given to UK athletes under 21 who 'accomplished the best performance at the AAA championships'.

John also won gold in the Commonwealth Games in 1970. In Sebastian Coe's closing address at the successful bid for the 2012 games, he described how, as a youngster in Sheffield, John and Sheila Sherwood had inspired him to pursue his successful career in athletics.

John Sherwood at Northern League Meeting, Gateshead 1976, 400 metres hurdles (York Press)

PHILIP NOEL-BAKER

One of the most famous old boys from York's Bootham School is Philip Noel-Baker, who was born in London in 1889. After school he went to Cambridge University. He began to compete in championships and this led to representing Great Britain in the Olympic Games in 1912, 1920 and 1924. It was in Antwerp in the 1920 games that he won the silver medal in the 1500 metres event. He served in the Friends Ambulance Corps during the war and earned decorations for valour. He later helped draft the covenant of the League of Nations, and went on to become Professor of International Relations at London University. He became an expert on disarmament and in the 1940s was Minister of State then Secretary of State for Air. In 1959, in recognition of his work and lifetime commitment to peace and on behalf of war refugees, he was awarded the Nobel Prize for Peace. He died in 1982.

WALTER WILKINSON

Walter Wilkinson was born in Harrogate in 1944 and came to York in 1959. He is recognised as one of the country's leading middle distance runners of the 1960s and '70s.

I was always interested, always quite good at running at school. When I was getting towards 14 and 15, I could run longer distances, I started running 880, half miles, gradually moved up to the mile which was possibly my most successful event. I ran in the Yorkshire Schools Championship and I won that.

Walter Wilkinson,
1960s

(Walter Wilkinson)

It really took off in 1959 when I started winning county championships and performing well in national schools championships. I think it took over my teenage years and beyond. You don't realise that you're getting obsessive, it just becomes a way of life. It's a matter of getting the balance right. Nervous energy can have a beneficial or an adverse effect. But then it's the excitement, you just get a flood of adrenaline. In those days, we didn't know much about diets. Looking back and seeing quite often I had a bit of inconsistency in performances, I could put it down to possible dehydration, in hot countries. You'd never dream of carrying a bottle of water around.

I joined Rowntree's Athletic Club, quite a successful club. York Harriers didn't have a track team. They were almost defunct. We used to train on their sports ground, Mille Crux up Haxby Road. There was a nice old guy who coached me, Ward Heath, who dedicated his whole life to athletics and coaching. He could go back to the days when York Harriers was a top club. I worked for the railway, I was a fireman and later a driver. They were always very good to me. Never any problems getting time off. They had the Staff Association and games at most levels. I always competed in regional and national level for them, mainly out of appreciation of the fact that they were so good.

Walter was the best runner at Rowntree's club.

I made a lot of friends at Rowntree's. Very important part of my athletic career. I won Yorkshire and North of England track and cross country championships on numerous occasions. Rowntree's was in one of the leagues. They've only recently become known as City of York Athletics Club. Not many of the members worked for Rowntree's, it was the only athletics club in York. We were purely amateurs. It was jolly difficult, working shifts and then running. The only advantage was that I could train in

Walter Wilkinson (number 1 on his vest), 1970 (Walter Wilkinson)

daylight hours in winter and summer, but it was tough going. There was no money in sport, you couldn't say, "I'm going to pack up my job and just race". It wasn't possible. Because you're a member of a club, you don't always train with them. I used to go out running round the streets of York, like people do nowadays. I was the only one doing it. As I was becoming more successful, Derek Ibbotson, a former world mile record holder, more or less poached me away to Longwith Harriers which had a group of good milers.

You graduate through country championships to Northern Counties. Then compete in national events. It can be quite a rapid progression to international level. I ran in the '66 Commonwealth Games in Jamaica. I finished fourth, just missed out on a bronze medal. It was the first major games that the Kenyans started to compete at. Obviously they've gone from strength to strength.

Walter was in line for the 1968 Olympics. He had been running very well and was due to compete in 1500 metres.

With Mexico being at altitude, we went over to Fuentemar in the French Alps a couple of times for pre-Olympic training.

Before going to Mexico, athletes had to have injections for tetanus, typhoid and paratyphoid.

Some people, it seemed to give them a kind of flu. It didn't affect me so I continued racing and lost my form. And that's all I can put it down to, having these injections and not realising that they'd affect my performance.

By losing his form, it meant that Walter was not able to compete in the Olympics.

The honour is being picked for the Olympics. The chances of winning a medal are very slim. You get a few, Mary Rand, Lynne Davis, Dorothy Hyman, Ann Packer. Seb Coe came on the scene towards the end of my career, 1976. I beat him in the trials for the Montreal Olympics but neither of us made the team. I was getting towards the end of my career by then. I carried on running until the 1980s. Then I used to run as a veteran up to about ten years ago.

The best time was probably winning the three A's champion-ships [in 1970]. *I ran my fastest mile in inter counties, the first Yorkshireman to win a sub-four minute mile in Yorkshire* [and the first under 21 in Britain]. *And I won a bronze medal at the*

European indoors one year. My fastest time was 3.56. I won most of my races running under four minutes. [Walter still holds the inter-county record over a mile].

Writing in the Telegraph in 2008, Sebastian Coe said

In early 1976, my senior apprenticeship began in earnest at the Yorkshire track championships, where I nicked across the line in the 1500 metres for my first senior title relegating the favourite, Walter Wilkinson, to runner-up.
Weeks later, when we were both selected to wear the white rose in the inter-counties championships at Crystal Palace, I got off the train at St Pancras and bumped into Wilkinson. Trying to make up for the impertinence of youth earlier in the month, I greeted him, 'Hello Walter. If I had known you were on the train I'd have come and sat with you'. 'On the train?', he said. 'I drove you down, you dozy ....' [as the train driver!]

AUDREY KILNER BROWN

Audrey Kilner Brown, MBE, (later Court), was born in 1913 in India. When her family returned to England, she ran with the Birchfield Harriers in London and won a silver medal in the 100 metre race in the 1936 Berlin Olympics. Her connection with York came when she lived in the city after the war, and worked as personnel officer at Rowntree's. She continued with athletics training and held classes for some of the women in the factory.

Interviewed for a book on women Olympians by Stephanie Daniels and Anita Tedder, she explained that,

I had four brothers who were all keen sportsmen and above average athletes. My parents never saw any difference between my taking up athletics and my brothers doing so.

In 1936, silver medallists were crowned with laurel wreaths.

Standing on the rostrum with the Canadians and Americans and looking round the vast stadium from this exciting point was the most important moment of the Games for me, despite wearing rather ridiculous oakleaf laurels.

I was always nervous at the start of a race because of my considerable deafness and fear of not hearing starters' orders. My hearing difficulty was not a severe one, just an inconvenience, but I found I could not relax sufficiently to be assured of a good start. People are more positive about disabilities now I am thankful to say.

Audrey captained the British women's team for the European championships in Vienna in 1938.

It was an unhappy political situation. We were in the city when the German government was making not-so-secret preparations for war. It was an intense relief to know that we had diplomatic protection as we were a small and vulnerable group of women, asked by the Foreign Office to compete as arranged.

DENIS JACKSON

Denis Jackson was born in York in 1945. Whilst working for the GPO, he began to compete in walking competitions, for Huntington Working Men's Club.

I did my first in 1968 and I won it in 1970. Nearly every working men's club had an annual walk, five miles. You'd get 80 or 90 from various clubs. It was a yacht handicap. The fastest goes off last. The first man would go, and 20 minutes later the last man. Everybody should come over the line together if they get it right.

Denis Jackson, York 1974 (Denis Jackson)

Some people are clumsy walkers and some people like rhythm. Fortunately I was a rhythm man.

At the Post Office they had a national 15 kilometre race walking championship. That's when I started to do other races within the Amateur Athletic Association. [In 1976] I got invited to go to Aldershot to train with the potential Olympic walkers. I started taking it more seriously. I was selected for my first international in 1980, in Paris. I'd train five or six days a week, 10 miles, 15 miles or 20 miles. I was a 50 kilometre international. It was a fantastic feeling. I'd go to work on a night and be like a Jack in a box, on a bit of a high, especially when I got in training.

When I look back, I must have been superfit. I used to eat anything and everything and never put weight on. Salt replacement drinks were just coming in, the first one was Staminaid. I'd drink water or flat Coke.

In 1981 Denis represented Great Britain in Spain and in January 1982 he was nominated for a Vaux Brewery Silver Star award.

Denis Jackson wins postman's walking race, 1970s (Denis Jackson)

My first [international] *I did in Valencia, the second in Bergen in Norway, third in the Isle of Man in 1985 and fourth in Central Park, New York. Then I decided I was going to retire and I went and watched the next one in Barcelona, wishing I was in it. So I made a bit of a comeback and got two more world championships, one in California and my last one in Monterey in Mexico. The British Amateur Athletic Board paid. They were really good. I'd trained hard and I was performing to the best of my ability. I was always in the top five.*

The only 'ill fated trip' was in 1982 when,

I went to Benidorm for two weeks. We were supposed to move on to Barcelona. We got a duff address from somewhere and couldn't find where the race was happening. We travelled up on a coach, it took about ten hours. We got to the place in Barcelona and they'd never heard of the race. So we spent the night sleeping out on the station.

But Denis's career went from strength to strength.

Denis Jackson congratulated by York Lord Mayor Ken Cooper 1984 (Denis Jackson)

My best time was 4 hours and 3 minutes, but now you can't get anybody to do 50 km in the time I used to do. It's not a glamour sport, I think you have to be a special breed. The working men's club thing was unique to York. If you wanted to walk anywhere else, you joined a walking club.

You go onto the road outside the stadium and do the last lap on the track and it's a lovely feeling coming into the stadium, with 40 or 50,000 people. I did a 35 km one at Brighton in '83, and I broke the British record. I was second in that race. I think it was my 37th birthday and it went in the Guinness Book of

Records for about three years. Britain was the top, in the '50s, '60s. Then Eastern Europeans and Mexican walkers came along, probably fulltime. They got better and better.

Denis was soon in line for the next Olympics.

1984, I always call it the budget Olympics. Los Angeles. There was two standards. The A standard, you had to do under four hours, three minutes. The B standard was four hours and ten minutes. I'd done four seven. I was waiting for my call. Every other year they'd taken the B standard, but for that one they only took the A standard, just one man, where they could have taken three.

It was in the 1980s that major concerns about drugs in sport came to the fore.

Every year you'd get a little booklet and it told you any medicines that contained anything illegal. Then if you were in the first three [in a race], *they'd take one out, and then they'd make their mind up to test number 3, number 7, and 17 or whatever. It could take you a long time to produce a sample because you get dehydrated.*

I have had injuries. [On one occasion] *I thought I'd torn a*

Denis Jackson, 1980s (Denis Jackson)

hamstring but it was a nerve.

Denis Jackson,
San Jose 1989.
World cup final
of 50 km walk.

(Denis Jackson)

I was off work for six or seven weeks. I went to see the Amateur Athletics Board physio at the international stadium at Gateshead. I'd put nearly a stone on in weight with not training and he said, "The best thing you can do is start training. I want you to get some anti-inflammatory drugs". And I went on them and it went.

They used to advise you to do two 50 km races a year. Sometimes I'd do three or four. I used to thrive on them. We had postman's walks as well, uniform walks. We still have one in York and one in London run by the Post Office Sports and Social Club. It was the 50th one in London last year.

Denis has dozens of cups from his walking career.

Every time I go to the postman's walk in London, I get at least three. I'm usually in the first three, and I usually get a veteran's one and get a team one. The ones for internationals, I keep them, there's a little story behind each one.

YORK SCHOOLS ATHLETIC ASSOCIATION

This association was founded in 1914, and held an annual sports festival in the city. At the annual meeting in 1966, general secretary Peter Wilmott, of Carr Junior School, said that the year

marks the end of 52 years of voluntary effort on the part of York's teachers to promote in the children under their charge, the physical, mental and moral development which comes from taking part in organised games and sports, and shows that the teachers of today are still very mindful of the aims laid down by the founders of the association.

Maureen Chevens was involved with the YSAA

from 1946 to 1955, while I was a pupil at Fishergate Junior then Mill Mount Grammar School, and from 1961 to 1974 when I was teaching at Mill Mount. Many primary and secondary schools were involved in the activities in York. Others went further and helped to take York pupils into county, national and international competitions.

A typical year in my diary is that of 1972, with YSAA committee meetings, swimming events, relay trials in May, first and second year high jumps, long jump, relay races, city schools sports heats for 200 metres, high jump, shot put. Then the county schools athletics in Hull, city schools sports heats in 100 metres, long jump, discus and javelin, then hurdles and relays. Swimming events in July and August, then in October preparing a report for the Guildhall, meetings and presentations, and in 1973 a York schools gymnastics competition for the first time.

When I was teaching at Mill Mount, we were asked to be part of a big display by York schools for a visit by the Queen on the

York Schools Athletics Association awards ceremony 1967 at Guildhall.
L to R – P N Willmott (Hon Secretary), Mrs Willmott, C S Baxter (Past President),
F W Lund (President), R Farnworth (Hon Treasurer), A C Pickering (Asst Hon Secretary).
(Maureen Chevens)

Knavesmire. My colleague Jean Gale and I were in charge of training and organising girl trampolinists because few other schools had been able to save up for a trampoline as we'd done. We were faced with taking the trampoline manually to the Knavesmire. The day was breezy and sunny but there were clouds and just before the Queen arrived we had a downpour, everyone was soaked. We looked like drowned rats rather than bright, cheerful and competent performers waiting to show our best work. The trampoline was soggy, about half the bounce the girls had been used to, and even when it eventually dried out, it was never the same again.

During my years as swimming secretary and joint secretary and treasurer for the athletics section with Jean Gale, we catered for at least 25 competing secondary schools in swimming and athletics, with a full programme of events, which meant a lot of work outside school time. Normal time meant for us not just lessons but also team practices, badminton, dancing, gym clubs, fencing, volleyball, inter-house matches, so the work for YSAA came on top of that but somehow it got done. We had a lot to be proud of at the end of it all.

(For more information, see the chapter on swimming).

SPECIAL OLYMPICS

The Special Olympics City of York Club was set up in 2007 for people with varying disabilities. The teams returned from the national Special Olympic Games in Leicester in 2009 with a total of 19 medals. This was a first for the York athletes and gold medals were awarded to Karl Mercer and Ann Pattison. 18 year old Joe Hadfield, and Laura Campbell, both from Applefields School, represented Great Britain in the 2010 Special Olympic European Summer Games in Warsaw. Laura won gold in tennis and Joe won silver for shot put and bronze for the 100 metre sprint.

MODERN PENTATHLON

The modern pentathlon is a variation on the military aspect of the ancient pentathlon, with the skills thought necessary to a cavalry soldier – swimming, fencing, running, riding and pistol shooting. It is considered to be the most difficult and testing of all international sports events.

GEORGE NORMAN

York man George Norman was a Company Sergeant Major instructor with the British army. In 1948 he was ninth in the inter-service pentathlon championships in Aldershot and chosen as a probable for the Olympic Games. But he was posted to the Gold Coast and entered no more competitions until 1951. He held the British Pentathlon title in 1953 and '54, and was a member of the three-man British team for the Melbourne Olympics in 1956. At that time riding, fencing, shooting, swimming and running took place over six days. Today the contest takes place in a single day.

TRIATHLON

The triathlon has only been part of the Olympics since 2000. In 2012 the event is to take place in Hyde Park, with a 1500 metre swim, 40km cycle ride and 10km run.

York Triathlon Club was founded in 2010. The club has had success at the national triathlon relay championships. Martin Harman of Heslington suffers from an abnormal heart condition yet has qualified for the European championships in Israel in April 2012. Rachel Lightfoot won gold in the world duathlon championship, competing with other club members Will Kaye, Sean McDermott and Terry Lightfoot.

ALAN RAYMENT

Unable to walk after losing both legs, Alan Rayment has been a member of the Great Britain elite paratriathlon squad since 2008. He is proving a real inspiration to others.

I'm the only person in Great Britain to teach studio cycling and boxercise, in a wheelchair. I never thought I would be able to do it. It gives a positive image to people who are disabled and think life is finished. It is not.

Alan has competed in the European championships and is working towards the World Cup.

I have been in the provisional squad for two years. Out of the 12 athletes selected, I was one of two who received an unconditional place. In 2016 I want to be in Rio racing in the Paralympics. It is definitely something I can achieve.

In May 2012, Alan is to go with a team to hand-cycle (using a special machine powered by the arms) 206 miles in six days across Eastern Europe, in aid of Romanian youth work. Alan received an honorary doctorate from York St John University and was voted 2011 Disabled Sports Achiever of the Year. He has taken part in numerous triathlons, the London marathon and has hand-cycled from Land's End to John O'Groats.

Alan Rayment receives an honorary doctorate from York St John University (York Press)

— Chapter 3 —
BADMINTON

Known originally as battledore and shuttlecock, and originating in India, the sport is thought to be named after Badminton in Gloucestershire, the home of the Duke of Beaufort, who championed the game in the 1870s. Badminton is the most recent of Olympic racquet sports. It was not awarded medals until 1992 and has been dominated by China though Britain won a silver medal in the mixed doubles in 2004.

It has been a popular sport in York for many decades. The Railway Institute was the first club to offer the game with one court in the gymnasium which opened in 1926. In 1946 this increased to four courts, and today there are nine, taking over the space previously used for indoor tennis. The 'Badminton Gazette' called the Railway Institute one of the best halls in the country. The wooden flooring has a small amount of grit in the varnish which gives a good grip. Although the Institute held 'restricted championships' in 1947, it did not offer full championships until 1960.

Badminton is considered to be an excellent way to keep fit. In a typical two game match, each player runs approximately one mile. After play was suspended over the war years, the York and District Badminton League was reformed in 1953 with men's and women's singles and doubles, and mixed doubles. In the 1960s, the League included teams from Rowntree's, the Railway Institute, Clifton, Malton, Stamford Bridge, Moor Lane, Yorkshire Schoolboys, the Amateur Deaf Association, St John's College, and York University. Clifton Badminton Club uses St Peter's School as well as the Energise Centre which has six courts with solid wood sprung floors.

PAUL HOBMAN

Paul Hobman began playing the game in the 1960s at the age of 14,

which is late really in badminton terms. I started at Tang Hall youth club, taught by a lady called Doris (Dot) Wood. Because they didn't have any facilities, we used the hall at Melbourne Youth Club, which was just big enough. The Youth Service [part of the City Council] *was run by Percy Roberts, an accomplished runner, good cricketer and footballer. He was keen that youth clubs would provide teams for the local league. So we played for a cup at the end of the season, mixed, men's and ladies, all in one session.*

Competitions ran during the winter months, playing teams from Scarborough, Knaresborough, Harrogate. I'd play with my wife-to-be and four others. The biggest accolade you could get, the

Youth Service colours, were presented at the Guildhall once a year. It was a cloth badge, a circular one, the city of York's emblem. Underneath was a flash for badminton or tennis or football or swimming. The Youth Service was very popular with youngsters. As you reached the magic age of 21, you were no longer allowed to represent a youth club.

Paul Hobman (Paul Hobman)

You then gravitated towards the York and District Badminton League. We formed Fulfordgate Badminton Club in 1972. I'm probably the last person left from the four or five who started the club.

You played with three pairs – nine rubbers, and the best of three games, so a match would last 27 games. We started playing at Fulford School, on a Tuesday, soon after seven. We had the hall until half past nine, ten o'clock. With only one court, we were stretched to get matches finished. Eventually we hired two courts at the Boys' Club in Lowther Street, then moved to Archbishop Holgate's, then to Lowfield School where we had four courts. People played social badminton on two courts and our matches would take the other two. About four years ago we moved to the Mount School and the facilities are much better.

It was 1800 when badminton started to be played, in India. It was the gentry who played in long trousers and long skirts [British military officers and their wives]. *Then it developed into a game where it is played at the most phenomenal speed. In the 1970s it became more popular because people had money to spend on leisure time and were more interested in keeping fit. Now there's two ladies divisions, three men's and seven mixed. York Railway Institute kept on winning everything, from 1953, until Moor Lane* [Club] *put a team together, that had Sue Fairley, an excellent player, and some other good players. They actually took the title away.*

John Bellerby is worthy of a mention, he has done a lot for York and District badminton, and Eileen McGarry.

Eileen McGarry, treasurer of the York League for many years, and deputy head of Margaret Clitherow School, died in 1974 and a trophy in her memory was provided.

John Bellerby, an amateur boxer, footballer and oarsman, became a keen badminton player from the 1950s to the 1980s. He was secretary of the Railway Institute badminton section from 1964 to 2007. He also established and ran a junior coaching evening, and helped to stage championships in York and Yorkshire. There is now an annual tournament competing for the John Bellerby trophy.

The game has also encouraged people with disabilities to become involved.

In Bootham, at the deaf school, one of the girls came down and joined our club, Jeannette. She was a great England international. We had competitions against them. We tend to get wheelchair users playing amongst themselves. I coach people at adult education. I teach kids from Fulford School at the university. The majority of other clubs, like the Railway Institute, have got the facilities to do it.

Shuttlecocks are normally referred to as feathers, originally they were a piece of cork with feathers stuck in and somehow bound with cord to keep them intact. The goose feathers would be spray lacquered. What you had then was very delicate so they weren't very durable. They are still expensive to buy. A dozen shuttlecocks will maybe cost £20. When badminton started to take off, manufacturers could see the viability of having a plastic shuttlecock which would be a lot more durable, instead of adding feathers for the skirt, a high impact plastic with a cork base. Blue rings indicate the speed of the shuttle. It's important to get the speed of the shuttle matched to the court. Manufacturers can cut the feathers to a certain angle which will speed the shuttle up or slow the shuttle down. The majority of the first division clubs play with feathered shuttlecocks. The rest of the clubs including my own have plastic shuttlecocks. Clubs allied to places like Rowntree's and the Railway get subsidies. It costs our club about £70 a night to hire a school hall for two and a half hours.

It's such a good social sport because it's played indoors during the winter months, usually most clubs will have social evenings. I'm still playing against people from when I started. And you can play into your 70s or 80s. You read about kids staying in their homes all weekend playing games online. It's sad because they're losing a lifelong enjoyment playing a sport such as badminton, tennis or squash. And all the nice people you meet, it enhances your social life.

— *Chapter 4* —
BASKETBALL

Basketball was first contested at the Olympic Games in 1936, though the first official game had been played in America in 1892, and that country has dominated the game. The Amateur Basketball Association of England and Wales was founded in 1936. The game is now one of the most popular and fastest growing sports worldwide. Wheelchair basketball, first created by disabled veterans after the Second World War, is played with specially designed chairs.

The sport is relatively new in York, but there are now teams at York College, York St John University and York University. Anne Morrice is Chair of the York Vikings Basketball Club, which was set up after a lottery-funded Millennium National Festival of Sport in 2000. It was preceded by a regional event in North Yorkshire with basketball as one of the sports on offer. Participants expressed a need for a York-based club. The club now has 59 boys and men (47 under 18), and 27 women and girls.

ANNE MORRICE

My involvement started in 2005 when my son started to play in Under 13s. At that point my only experience had been seeing the Harlem Globetrotters play. One of the great things about York Vikings is that it's a community club, run by parents or volunteers. I got involved as team manager, spent some time as club secretary and now I'm the Chair.

Because of my son's involvement, I, along with other parents, qualified as a table official. Some are Level 1, some are Level 2.

That's the way of keeping the cost down, we do the table offi-ciating on a voluntary basis. And I'm a Level 2 coach. You do get to know the game a lot better and see it and watch it in a different way.

Girls have the option of netball as well so it can be harder to get girls' teams going. The ones who do play really love it. It's a dynamic game, very fast moving, and very much geared to attacking and scoring points so there are strict time limits at each stage of the game. If the team has possession at their end of the court, they only have eight seconds to get it into the other half and 24 seconds from having gained possession to trying a shot. If they haven't attempted to score, then posses-sion is handed over to the other team. They get five seconds to throw the ball if they have got sideline possession. If you're an attacking player you can only stay near the basket for three seconds so you can't have people crowding out the area. They have to keep moving.

There is a very healthy York and District Schools Basketball Association. One of the teachers will take responsibility each year for organising schools fixtures. Bootham School has just won the Under 14s final this year. So they'll be going forward to the Yorkshire final. And we've got national league involvement [to be able to compete on a regional basis]. *What I would like to see more is a level in between those who enjoy playing it and the national league players who train two hours twice a week and play a game at the weekend. That's a big commitment.*

Obviously the fees are based on the cost of hiring the court and the cost of participating. We have to pay referees for national league games. You can only take 12 players to a match so selec-tions need to be made. The game has five players on court at any one time but there can be rolling substitutions, so it is possible that all twelve get some game time. It's on the basis of how well an individual might be playing and their strengths compared to the opposition, and how the team dynamics are working for the opposition and our team. If there's a big difference in the scores that isn't going to be changed by the end, you might use that opportunity to give some of your less experienced players some experience.

There are four quarters each of ten minutes but the game can take a lot longer to play. Every time the ball goes out of bounds the clock stops. Home matches (and training) are mainly at York College although sometimes at Manor School. Our ladies and girls and under 12s train at Burnholme.

This year the under 14s will have played 20 games. They will have gone up to Newcastle, to Leeds and down as far as Shef-field. I go to all of the matches that my son's involved in. The under 14s, 16s and 18s compete in the national league and the men and the women compete in the local league. They've not been training together for as long.

Wheelchair basketball started last year and we had a grant from the Great Britain Wheelchair Association. The rules are largely the same. Until you get to a certain level, you can have mixed teams, some able bodied players in a wheelchair as well. Once you get to a certain level, you have a points system. According to the disability, each player has a points rating. You are allowed a certain number of points on court at any one time. You can also play inclusive zone basketball, with an equal number of running players and wheelchair players on each team. We were running sessions last year for adults and juniors but we've got a problem with venue availability so we're working on getting that re-established for this year.

York Vikings basketball *(York Vikings)*

They shoot at a ten foot basket, so their upper body strength is just immense. When you see four or five wheelchairs all converging on a ball and they're bending down to scoop it up again, it takes a certain amount of courage. The sports wheelchairs are amazing, very lightweight and extremely manoeuvrable. The wheels are at an angle to give them more stability and they have a tip mechanism to stop them going right over at the back, although there is a foul in wheelchair basketball because certain players will try and get the footplate of their chair under the footplate of the other player's chair and knock them off balance. It's a very intense sport.

City of York Council is very committed to providing more opportunities for people to play sports at all levels. It was quite interesting in some of our start up sessions when some of our running basketball players also came, to see how they have the basketball skills but not the wheelchair controlling skills. Some of the wheelchair players obviously had both. It's been good fun. The wheelchair users playing basketball very quickly establish their credentials in terms of their skill levels. Just as a running player has to run dribbling the ball, you can't carry it, the same applies to wheelchair basketball players, they can't just put the ball on their knee, they are allowed two turns of the wheel then they have to bounce it again.

The cost of the sport is a definite issue. Once you look at hire charges, it's not cheap. We do have some outdoor facilities, Rowntree's Park and Glen Gardens [and West Bank Park]. *It's dependent on the weather. It's a very attractive sport because it can be played on so many levels. You can play it just one on one, shooting hoops, or get a few friends together and you can play two or three people. It's very adaptable.*

But it's the role of volunteers in keeping these clubs going. Our club secretary is going to be carrying the Olympic torch, Hilary Campbell, the day before it arrives in York. The club will be involved in the event on the Knavesmire. And I'm volunteering at the Paralympics, with the basketball technical team.

— *Chapter 5* —
BOXING

Great Britain has won 48 medals for boxing in the Olympics, including 14 gold. In 1908 all three heavyweight boxing medallists came from Britain.

Anthony Power, York Olympic fencer, and later physiotherapist to the British swimming team, worked with British boxers at the 1980 Olympics.

> *We shared a camp at Crystal Palace with the boxing team. They didn't have a physio and I was very interested in boxing because it was closer to my particular sport, a combat sport. So I went to a lot of the fights and tried to help people in between bouts if they had any injury problems. Boxing and fencing are very similar, two guys, make your own decision, stand or fall by the decisions you make. Fencing comes from public school, army, club tradition. The culture is completely different but the sports are similar. You either find it exciting or you don't. Amateur boxing is very carefully regulated, a true sport with people equally matched in very carefully controlled situations.*

Boxing has a history of being a popular form of entertainment in York, reaching back several centuries. Much of it was illegal, and took the form of bare knuckle fighting. In the fairs which came to St George's Field, there were booths for boxing and wrestling, and locals were challenged to go three rounds with the champion and win a prize if they could knock him down, which rarely happened.

Beween the two world wars, there were a number of good boxers in the city. The Yorkshire Evening Press in an article in 1978, described Harry Ainsworth and Joe Routledge as 'two outstanding men who gave classic displays', and mentioned boxers Jack Stephenson, Joe Groves, Bot Andrews, Fred Mereweather and the Hawksby Brothers, who 'all fought for peanuts compared with present day purses. They were the so-called bread and butter fighters'. As York was a military base, the city also attracted some good army boxers in the 1930s.

The York Health and Strength Club paid five shillings a week to hire a room at the Five Lions. In February 1921, the York Boxing and Physical Training Club opened at the Londesborough Hotel in Petergate, with a rent of 2s 6d a week.

BOY WATSON

Joss Watson, known as Boy Watson, was one of York's most famous boxers of the 1920s. He was a flyweight who fought many of the top boxers of his era including Tiger Smith

Joss (Boy) Watson with son Geoffrey, 1940

(Janet Pigott)

Cartoon of Boy Watson 1940s

(Janet Pigott)

from Sheffield, to whom he lost on points in a memorable event at the Festival Concert Rooms. He was also a keen soccer player and played for Scarcroft School, York City Boys, and Rowntree's minors. He married Doris Pritchard in 1933 and died in 1972.

GEORGE AND HARRY KILDIN, AND MANAGER CHARLES 'PADDY' RYAN

George Frederick (known as Fred) and Harry Kildin were two York boxing brothers. Harry was a schoolboy Amateur Boxing Association champion. One of Fred's early tournaments, representing the York Railway Institute, was at the Montague Burton Amateur Boxing Club in Leeds in 1954 when he was 22. A year later, both brothers competed in the heavyweight category at a tournament in Saltaire, Fred as a senior and Harry as a junior, weighing eight stone. Fred was named the East and West Riding of Yorkshire champion in 1956.

Fred Kildin, 1950s (Heather Kirby)

Harry Kildin, 1950s (Heather Kirby)

The brothers were successful at a match in Saltaire where Fred, billed as the Railway Heavyweight, defeated M Garber of the Gold Coast. After being down in the first round, he made a great recovery and won clearly. Both boxers were given a tremendous ovation. This was Fred's second victory in a week.

By 1959, the brothers had changed their names to Freddie and Harry Kaye and were boxing as far afield as Hartlepool, Walsall and Leicester. An agreement in October 1959 between Fred and promoters Jack and Arthur Green of Leeds, stated that an appearance at Leeds Town Hall on 8th December 1959 in a contest of six rounds of three minutes against Nan Halah of Tonga, would result in payment of £15. If the contest were televised, the promoter would pay the boxer 23¾ per cent of the remuneration.

By the 1950s, boxing was strictly regulated by the British Boxing Board of Control, and boxers had to apply each year for renewal of a licence

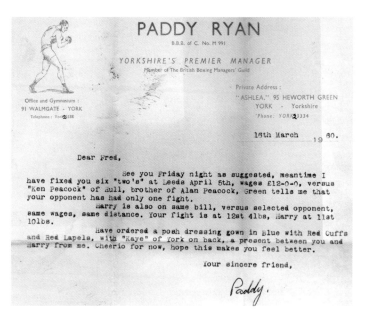

Letter to Fred Kildin from Paddy Ryan, 1960

(Heather Kirby)

which cost £1. These had to be carried at all times, and inspectors were requested to check them at tournaments. A letter in June 1956 advised boxers that, '*A properly fitting Gum Shield is an important part of a boxer's equipment, but it is of vital importance that it should fit properly. An ill fitting Gum Shield does much more harm than good, and the Medical Committee strongly recommend that the practice of buying ready-made Gum Shields should cease. The amount of 20s to 25s that a competent dentist will charge for making one is well worth spending*'.

A letter to all boxers and managers from the Board in 1959, explained a new regulation, '*requiring boxers to have available at least two pairs of boxing trunks of different colours. Several reports have been received of boxers turning up at tournaments with only one pair. Boxers are warned that failure to have two pairs of trunks will render them liable to disciplinary action*'.

The brothers were managed by promoter Charles 'Paddy' Ryan of Heworth Green, who had his gymnasium at 91 Walmgate.

Unfortunately Paddy Ryan died suddenly in September 1960. He was only in his 40s, and owned two footwear businesses in Goodramgate and Walmgate. His obituary stated that he was ' A good flyweight in his native Liverpool in his younger days, he put York back on the boxing map after the last war when he became a manager, teaming up with Vince Capaldi as trainer and handler. Their boxers fought in practically every hall in the country and included Con (Kid) Bailey, Harry Ainsworth, Reg Mortimer, Danny Delaney, Arty Dale, and Harry Allison. Ryan helped to stage open air tournaments on York Rugby League Club's ground at Clarence Street, a few years ago'.

Fred Kildin's career came to an end in 1960 but his brother Harry continued boxing until 1968, with a total of 21 bouts.

York Boxing Club was formed in 1967 in North Street, moving later to a gym in Fifth Avenue, and then to the Olympia Club in Selby. The club has produced 31 champions at club and national level, and seven professionals. Henry Wharton started his career at York before he moved to Leeds. He fought Nigel Benn, Chris Eubank and Robin Reid in world title fights. In 2004 the club became a registered charity. It now has an education department, 'Off the Hook'. Henry Wharton is in the process of transforming the top floor of the old Regent Cinema in Acomb into the Eastside Boxing Club and fitness centre, which will be the biggest club the city has ever had. Wharton is an undefeated super middleweight champion in European and commonwealth status.

FRANK FOWLER

One of the best known boxers in England in the 1920s, was York man Frank Fowler. He was born in 1906, and started his boxing career in 1921. Within a short time he was fighting in London, Manchester and other big cities, and then travelling all over Europe. The Ring magazine stated, *'Frank Fowler inspired more respect for British boxing on the continent than any fighter before or since. He beat more official champions of European countries than any other British boxer'*. And this record has never been broken.

At one famous fight in 1927, he beat the light heavyweight champion of Britain, Billy 'Gypsy' Daniels. The Daily Mirror reported 'Gypsy Daniels of Wales, light heavyweight champion of Great Britain, was beaten on points by Frank Fowler'. Although Fowler beat many champions, he did not get a title, 'the champion without a crown'. He sent shock waves through the game by outpointing newly crowned light heavyweight champion Tom Berry, at Liverpool Stadium in 1925, when he was 18.

Fowler's best ever performance was his points win over the French champion Maurice Griselle at Newcastle in 1930. He quit boxing at the age of 25 with over sixty fights under his belt.

Frank Fowler beats Gypsy Daniels (Norman Fowler)

His son, Norman Fowler, well known as singer Steve Cassidy, recalls,

He was always interested in boxing from being a schoolboy. He started when he was about 13, and he turned professional when he was 16. He used to tell the tale that when he was at school, he did a paper round and a gang of boys set on him and beat him up. So he waited for each one in turn when they were on their own and he got his own back.

The Festival Concert Rooms was at the back of the Assembly Rooms. They used to stage boxing matches. He fought there. There were one or two pubs in York that had training facilities. The Londesborough had a ring at the back. But he'd train at the Railway Institute. He said they built the running track round the top of the gym, like a balcony, for him. He'd train in heavy boots and run to make his legs strong. Boxing really saps your energy. You have to be very fit. He was very strong. About 12 and a half stone is about the maximum for a light heavyweight boxer.

He used to talk about one fight in particular, at Newcastle Free Trade Hall. He was supposed to fight Phil Scott who was heavyweight champion of the world. My father was a light heavyweight and if he'd beaten him, he would have been a world champion. But Scott cried off, he was ill or something, so another chap who was a good boxer, fought, and there were huge crowds there, they had to be controlled by police on horses.

He fought in Turin in Italy, a monte-velodrome where they'd test Fiat cars on top of the building. By the time he was 21 he'd beaten loads of European champions. He was never champion because they were catch-weight contests and they weren't at championship weight. Gypsy Daniels beat Max Schmeling who became world champion, and my father beat Gypsy Daniels. Max Schmeling wouldn't fight my father, I think he'd heard he was pretty good, and would avoid him. Father didn't have a proper manager, my mother

Lonz Webster, Frank Fowler and brother
Laurey Fowler 1930s (Richard Fowler)

managed his fights. Sometimes you were on a percentage of the gate and you could be cheated by unscrupulous people. So my mother would count the people, so he got his share of the gate money. He fought in The Ring in London which was a famous venue. It was bombed during the war but there's a pub called The Ring and my father's picture is up there. It was glamorous, women would go dressed up to watch the fights. You could have a meal ringside in evening dress.

Boxing poster, 1931, with Frank Fowler top of the bill (Richard Fowler)

Lonz Webster, 'the cast iron Scot' was a friend of his, the swimming coach. You could see he'd been a boxer. My father never had cauliflower ears. He was very handsome when he was young. When they get their ears banged, like at rugby, after you come off it's all swollen up, and it looks like a cauliflower ear immediately. But [to avoid that] *you just let the water out, push a needle into it. He didn't look like a typical boxer. I think it was because he didn't let people hit him very often. He had a good left hand, which is very good because you keep the opponent away with your left hand. He did have a lot of bouts and he used to fight 12 or 13 rounds. They'd fight with lightweight gloves, used to bandage their hands as boxers do still and then put the gloves on outside the ring, and many boxers would break the horse-hair in the gloves. Now they put the gloves on in the ring so*

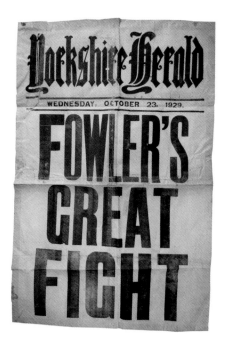

Yorkshire Herald board advertising Frank Fowler's fight, 1929 (Richard Fowler)

that there's no funny business. He was injured inasmuch as his memory was damaged by boxing. He couldn't remember sometimes what he did yesterday but he could remember all his fights and things in the past. Now they have to wear head protection in amateur boxing and in the Olympics as well which is a good thing. Of course they don't in professional boxing.

I know what a classic style boxer he was. He would spar in a mirror, shadow boxing, you stand in front and practise your punches. So you can see where the gaps are, where you might be letting somebody punch you. One man paid a lot of money to see him fight. He got in and my father's fight had just started and he put his hat underneath his seat and when he looked up, my father had knocked [his opponent] *out so he never saw it.*

Even in my father's day there was booth fighting at fairgrounds. At least boxing now they have to be physically fit and checked by doctors and there's a doctor on call if they do happen to be knocked out. Quite late in his career, he'd been sparring in Bridlington. There was a wall on one side of the boxing ring too near the ropes and he bounced into the ropes and hit his head on the wall behind it, just covered in canvas. My mother said that when he came back from that training session, he looked terrible. And she thinks that did the damage. It's usually not the punch but when they hit their head on the floor in the ring, that's quite often when some boxer's been badly hurt. Now the referee has got to intervene when he realises that somebody's hurt. He's got to stop the fight. Sometimes they don't.

My brother did box, went on nearly for Olympic standard but then he signed professionally for York and played rugby. I boxed a bit at school and the only time I was ever mentioned in our school magazine, I went to St Michael's at Leeds, was because I boxed at Stonyhurst and beat my opponent then. Then I started singing and I realised that people don't hit you back when you're singing, not very often anyway.

Francis Richard Fowler is Frank's oldest son, born in 1941. He explains,

When he boxed in York, it was usually in the Festival Concert Rooms opposite the public library, the only venue which would hold the number of people. A lot of the bigger fights were in London, Liverpool, Manchester or Newcastle. Newcastle had a massive population because it was a big ship building and steel making area. They used to get 10,000 to 12,000 at the fights.

My mother said the nearest person she'd ever seen to how he used to box, was Cassius Clay [Muhammad Ali]. *He danced round and made the other person look a complete mug. A fighter and a boxer are different. A boxer is a man who stands and boxes and picks his punches and walks around, an artist, a bit like Clay used to fight. A fighter is a chap who goes in and just throws punches haphazardly. So he can land a lucky punch. A good boxer will always beat a good fighter. All he's got to do is stand and hold them*

Ticket to Frank Fowler fight at Festival Concert Rooms, York, 1929.(Richard Fowler)

Frank Fowler, 1920s
(Norman Fowler)

off. A fighter just hopes he can land one lucky punch, whereas a boxer can dance around and defend himself and pick up points. My father was a very good dancer. He'd win competitions at places like Blackpool or Bournemouth. There was nobody in comparison, the amount of people who he beat, from all over Europe. He would travel all over, by train, by boat, to places to fight. There was nobody to touch him. Even now he doesn't get the recognition.

His father was a bit dubious of all the people that were on the go. He knew there were so many gangsters who were running boxers, and he didn't want his son to go into this. My mother used to write off for fights for him to different places, and put articles in the paper to challenge people. She'd get him fights for £250, which was a lot of money when you could buy a house for £200. You had to pay for sparring partners and masseurs and corner men. When my father retired, they wanted him to take over at St Peter's and be sports master, but he wasn't interested.

Frank Fowler died in 1981. In his latter years, he was shown in a newspaper article with a letter from America addressed to 'Frank Fowler, York Boxer, England', which says it all.

— Chapter 6 —
CANOEING

The sport of canoeing is divided into slalom and sprint. The latter was first contested in the Olympics in 1936, but slalom only began in 1972. After a twenty year break it returned as a sport in 1992. Two types of boats are used, canoes for one or two competitors, and kayaks for up to four. Britain won bronze in Athens in 2004 in the women's K1 (kayak) singles event. In the 2008 Olympics Britain won gold in the 1000 metres men's singles, and bronze in the men's 500 metres.

The first mention of canoeing in York is of the York Canoe Club in 1974. It now has 183 members, and a boathouse by the river off Almery Terrace, where members meet during the summer. After their time on the river, they often relax in the Bay Horse, Marygate. The club runs an 'Introduction to Paddling' course for first timers, teaching the basics of canoeing. Members paddle all over England, Wales and Scotland, and spend weekends in the Dales and Lake District. Some members have paddled in France, Austria, Canada, Turkey, USA and Uganda.

There is also the York University Canoe Club, which uses kayaks rather than canoes. In summer they spend time surfing at the seaside. The Lower Wharfe Canoe Club based at Tadcaster has been running since 2000, with a base at Tadcaster Community Swimming Pool and at Bishopthorpe on the River Ouse. The club works with anyone from beginners to advanced whitewater kayakers.

TOM QUINN

Tom Quinn was born in York in 1991. He is a member of the Great Britain Under-23 Squad and has his sights set on competing in the

2012 Olympic Games. He has been British National Junior Champion three times, English National Senior Champion, British University Champion in three classes, Junior and Under-23 finalist and Under-23 silver medallist. In 2011, at an inter-university slalom event, Tom won three golds in the C1 class, C2 and the team event. He also won gold and bronze in the premier division race in Bala, North Wales. At the Under 23-selection event, he took first and third place to go forward to the European championships.

I grew up in Bishopthorpe. I went on a watersports day with the Bishopthorpe Cubs and one thing we tried was canoeing. I really really enjoyed it. I joined the Lower Wharfe Canoe Club after a bit of pestering of my mum to let me. I quickly outgrew the pool so started slalom. I got spotted by George Stephenson, who did the slalom. And then he kind of pushed me and I progressed from that.

I chose Nottingham University so I could train at the National Watersports Centre. . My life is very orientated around canoeing. I am training six days a week for about four hours a day, possibly more.

Tom has been spending time at Lee Valley in Hertfordshire, which will be the scene of the 2012 canoeing competition.

It's an absolutely amazing facility, just really motivating me to get to the Olympics. It's like nothing else we've got in the UK.

Tom feels very grateful for the support he gets from home.

Bishopthorpe Parish Council has been very supportive, they sponsored me. It's been invaluable. My parents are absolutely phenomenal. Lots of people have contributed as well which has kept me going. I'm just onto my third new boat. They are so

Tom Quinn, 2011 (Tom Quinn)

expensive. My boats are worth more than my car is. [A new C1 boat costs £1400, paddles cost £170, and buoyancy equipment is £500 a year. There are also transport costs and entry fees to be found]. *In kayaks, you sit down, closed cockpit, and you have a two bladed paddle, whereas with a C1 it's still a closed cockpit but you kneel down and you have a single bladed paddle.*

The university have also been very good at supporting me. They've allowed me to train effectively. I want to achieve my educational aspirations as well as sporting ones. As well as 2012, I'm thinking ahead to 2016 in Rio and beyond.

Canoeing is an exciting sport to watch, but to do it, especially on some of the courses like Lee Valley, nothing compares to it, the adrenalin, the buzz you get. The Junior Europeans were in Solkan in Slovenia, Slovakia and last year in Bosnia. The Under-23 world championships this year are in America. That will be a very exciting experience.

Tom is seen as an inspiration to local young people. He has been into his old primary school in York to talk to the pupils about setting achievable goals and really wants to encourage other young people to take up the sport.

— Chapter 7 —
CYCLING

Olympic cycling is split between road and track events. In 1996 mountain biking was added to the programme, as well as BMX racing in 2008. British teams have always done relatively well but enjoyed unprecedented success in Beijing in 2008 with 14 medals, eight of them gold. Chris Hoy is the first British man to win three golds at one Games, and Rebecca Romero is the first British woman to win medals in two different sports, cycling and rowing, in 2004.

Lawrence Street Sunday School cycle club 1890 (City of York Council, Local Studies Collection)

York's love affair with cycling really began towards the end of the 19th century. Cycling then was both recreational and a means of transport, as it has continued to be, despite the advent of the automobile. In 1877 the York Bicycle Club was founded. The Yorkshire Gazette of October 1878 reported a successful series of races held by the club at the Yorkshire Gentlemen's Cricket Ground, with six events competing for 'valuable prizes'. There were 50 entrants. The handicap mile race was won by J L Varley who received a 'handsome timepiece', with second prize, 'a fine inkstand' going to J J Krous.

Priory Street men's class cycle club 1890s (York Oral History Society)

York City and Suburban Bicycle Club, one of the oldest clubs in the country, was founded in 1879. Its meetings were held at 2 Coney Street, attracting both male and female members. Clubs often held 'smokers' where members would get together for smoking and entertainment, with the clay pipes often supplied by the landlord of the inn where they met.

There were about 50 cycling clubs in York and the surrounding area at the beginning of the 20th century, including York Harriers (more often associated with athletics), which held its first 'cycling gymkhana' in 1903, York Layerthorpe and District Cycling Club and Lawrence Street Sunday School Cycling Club. In April 1902, Dent's of Stonegate were advertised as 'The cream of the Cycle Agencies, Best place for Expert Repairs. Hiring machines by day, week or months'.

After the Second World War, the city still had seven cycling clubs, the Clarion, Ebor Cycling Club, York Olympics, Derwent Valley Wheelers, York Phoenix, Clifton Cycling Club and a branch of the national Cyclists' Tourist Club.

CLARION CYCLING CLUB

In 1929, four York men, Alex McTurk, Harold Raven, Bert Hepple and Mr Helliwell, formed the Clarion Cycling Club, a branch of the national club which had been founded in 1894 in Birmingham. The club had had an Easter meet in York in 1913, attracting 1000 Clarion cyclists from all over the country. There were several more Clarion meets in the city, before a York branch was formed. Harold Raven recalls,

> *I was 15 in 1929, we met at Alex McTurk's house in Charlton Street. Our first outing was to Pontefract and Ferrybridge. After that we extended our distance to Scarborough and Whitby. We formed three sections, the higher riders, 150 miles onwards, the day riders, up to 100 miles, and the afternoon riders. About a third were women. There were some good friendships made. It got so big that one or two members broke away and formed the Ebor Cycling Club.*

> *We rode in twos, the captain at the front, sub captain at the rear, and one in between keeping formation. With 70 cycles, you had 35 pairs which covered a fair distance, quite difficult for vehicles to overtake. We used to have ports of call, one was Ma Green's at Scagglethorpe, coming back from the coast. We were*

Alex McTurk 1912 (Van Wilson)

67

Alex McTurk, 1948
(Van Wilson)

made welcome there, tea and cakes were very reasonable. The other was Gregson's of Thirsk. He had a penny farthing and it was there for anybody who wanted a ride.

The Clarion call was 'Boots', as a recognition for other members. [One group would shout this and the answer was 'Spurs']. *In summer we wore shorts and an open necked shirt and in winter we had plus fours and polo necks. There were two prominent dealers in York – Freddy Fenton and Arnold Elsegood. Fenton built his bikes, the Fenton Five, and the Fenton Zip. They could be built to your own specification.*

We went to Halifax to a meeting, and when we sat down, first one started itching then another, then one took his pants off and started shaking them in the wind and ten yards away the women were doing likewise. We'd sat down on anthills.

Freddie Fenton,
Mrs Fenton with
baby Marion on
the Fenton Zip bike
(Mike Race)

I went off to Whitby once and the Sleights Bridge was broke down and the bridge washed away with floods. We decided to go to Bridlington as an alternative. By the time we got back, we'd had a longish day and were a bit saddle sore, but you'd think nothing of going on a bike in those days.

Although the Clarion Club folded in York, it continues nationally.

Clarion Cycling Club, Blubberhouses
Moor 1930 (York Oral History Society)

Clarion Cycling Club at teashop in Pocklington
1930s (York Oral History Society)

PETER LONGBOTTOM

Peter Longbottom was the first York man to complete the Milk Race (Tour of Britain, which began in 1944) in 1981. Although born in Huddersfield, most of his life was spent in York. In 1979, at the age of 21, as a member of the York Denison Cycling Club, he was chosen to cycle for Great Britain in the World Amateur Road Race Championships in Holland and again in 1983 in Switzerland.

As a result of this he was shortlisted for selection for the 1980 Olympic Games but did not make the final squad. In 1981 he won bronze in the national 100 mile time trial championships. He retained his title in the British team for the 1982 Milk Race, and won the Ryedale sportsperson of the year trophy in November of the same year. His first Commonwealth medal was a bronze in 1990 and in the 1994 Commonwealth Games in Canada he won silver in the 100 kilometres time trial. Peter was a member of the York club Velo by this time. At the age of 33, he was finally chosen for the Olympics, one of the oldest cyclists to represent Britain, at the Games in Barcelona in 1992.

Sadly, Peter died tragically in 1998, at the age of 38 when a car hit his bicycle near the Grimston bypass. Cyclists from around the world attended the funeral. He was described as 'a true professional who inspired cyclists all over the world'. Several years later the Peter Longbottom Memorial Trophy was given to riders in the Yorkshire Regional Road Race Championships.

CLIFTON CYCLING CLUB

Clifton Cycling Club, which is still flourishing today, was founded in 1895 when its inaugural meeting took place at the Old Grey Mare. The winter of that year was a very bad one, and the Ouse froze to a depth of several inches. Two club members rode from York to Poppleton on the ice by tandem. Early photographs show male riders in shirts, ties and jackets, with the ladies wearing long dresses and big hats.

Clifton Cycling Club 1895 (York Oral History Society)

Clifton Cycling Club sign (Peter Burbidge)

The first full female member in 1923 (and later president) was Kate Green. Despite wearing what would now be considered an old-fashioned outfit, her photograph was banned by Cycling Weekly as being indecent. During the Second World War, the club held Sunday afternoon rides for anyone, as part of York's 'Holidays at Home'.

ROY CROMACK, PETER SMITH, JOHN WATSON

In 1968, three members of Clifton Cycling Club, Roy Cromack, Peter Smith and John Watson, were chosen to go to the Mexico Olympics. It was unusual for three members of a single club to be in the squad. The trio competed in the 100 kilometres event.

York Olympic cyclists, L to R – Pete Smith, John Watson, Roy Cromack.
(*York Oral History Society*)

Though born in Doncaster in 1940, Roy Cromack moved to York and joined the club. He represented Great Britain in track races and the international Peace Race and won medals at every distance in British time trial championships. He was the first British cyclist to ride more than 500 miles in a 24 hour time trial in 1969, in what was described as 'an inspired ride'.

Pete Smith rode in the world championships and won the 'King of the Mountains' jersey in the Tour of Morocco. In the Press, Pete explained about the trio's Olympic appearance.

We only had a few months to prepare, we were all amateurs and had proper jobs, I was a joiner, John was a builder and Roy was a teacher. We trained on evenings and weekends, riding 50 kilometres each time. The conditions took some getting used to because of the rarefied atmosphere. There were worries athletes would die! The thin atmosphere benefited the shorter distances. It wasn't the case for the cycling. Each team has four cyclists in a line, each sheltering the next man from the wind, changing positions riding at the front for a while, taking the wind, then switching to the back. There's nothing like the opening ceremony and actually being there when the 800 metre runner runs up and lights the flame. The whole arena goes absolutely silent. It's a really moving atmosphere, you can't relate what it's like to anybody.

John Watson of the York builders, H Watson & Son, of Heworth, was the third member of the York trio. In 1970, representing Clifton Cycling Club, he won the annual British Best all Rounder competition.

PETER BURBIDGE

Peter Burbidge was born in York in 1935.

My first recollection of cycling anywhere in the York area – Coxwold and Helmsley and Rievaulx Abbey and that was the latter end of our school days. In 1950 I started seriously. I'd gone to my cousin's wedding and there was a very nice looking young lady there. She was with the Ebor Cycling Club. Her husband was a cyclist but I wasn't to know that. She said, "Do you do any?" I said, "Funnily enough I have just bought a new carbon bike, marvellous machine". "Why not come and have a ride with us?" I went to Clifford's Tower where the Ebor Cycling Club used to meet. When I arrived, there was this chap with her about six foot tall. And I realised I'd better stick to cycling because there's me at about five foot six at the time.

In York when I first started you had the Ebor, the Clifton, the Clarion, the Phoenix which was the racing side of the CTC touring club, and the St Christophers who always went to St Wilfred's first and set off after church service. In the '50s fellas started to afford a motorbike or even a little car so they were moving away from cycling.

We had an inventors club in the Ebor. Some of the lads worked at Vickers Instruments. Two of them, Dave and Geoff, made their own spear guns, about a foot long, for shooting, spearing fish under water. They decided to strap these under the crossbar. I think they were trying to empty the sea around Land's End. We got to Lynmouth and it was flooded. We had to make our way back to York with spear guns on the back of the bikes. I only toured with a small saddlebag, some of them had panniers. I used to find a youth hostel during our fortnight out and would have a parcel posted with all fresh gear in, and post my old stuff back.

One day they decided we would build a big sledge and put two bike wheels on, one either side. When we wanted to use it, we could uncouple the wheels and we had a sledge big enough for three full-grown chaps. We could have gone to the top of Terrington Bank, it's good sledging. But no, our idea was to tow this heavy sledge to Fridaythorpe, over the top of Garrowby Hill. When it was my turn to do so many miles, it included

Garrowby Hill. I set off with this big heavy sledge behind me. There's a safety slip road and I somehow or other ended up there with the bike and the sledge on top. That was absolutely crazy.

On one occasion Pete and two friends rode back from London in one day.

We'd stopped at Highgate youth hostel. With me was the best rider in Yorkshire, or certainly in the top three, the late John Stiger. We'd no money left, we'd been away for a fortnight. We had to make it in a day. We did it!

I think the hardest ride I ever did and the one I'm most proud of was a time trial with Ebor Cycling Club, I would be 18 or 19. We set off at midnight and rode through the night to the Lake District, 90 mile out, and back, and crossing the Pennine chain twice, so it's hard, you're climbing. Basically, time trialling,

Cycling Club annual dinner 1956, Peter Burbidge in middle at front, holding cup. (Peter Burbidge)

you try to beat a clock all the time, set off at minute intervals.
I would sooner be in a road race trying to beat other people. A
lot comes into that, sitting in, breaking away, knowing your
moments. I enjoyed the place-to-place rides.

The Ebor Cycling Club broke up when many of its members had to go
off to do national service for two years. Peter and his wife joined the
Clifton Cycling Club which,

had a nucleus of older people who'd come back from the war,
to keep the club going. And it had much younger members. They
had behind them men like Arnold Elsegood who used to own the
cycle shop on Lord Mayor's Walk which is now Trotter's [now
in partnership with Giant]. *He was a brilliant frame builder.*
[He also set up the York Bicycle Polo League, and a tandem club
which included some blind members.]

On the Easingwold road, they start at the Blacksmith's Arms.
Up to 15 years back, we were racing that road to Thirsk, 12 ½
mile out, 12½ mile back. To do that you needed police permis-
sion to ride your course, the management of your time keeper,
time keeper's assistant, marshals, volunteers to man the junc-
tions. On that road today you'd need a line of ambulances. It
would be suicide to do it.

One of our club members who rode the Tour de France and also
the North Yorkshire Road Club member, was Vin Denson [who
lived in York in the 1960s]. *In the road racing, you have a team*
of riders and among them you have a star man. That star man
will have other riders round him act as 'domestiques', who will
take the front for him, shelter their number one man. Riding
behind one another is slipstreaming. Like you see geese flying
in arrow form, it makes a big difference. Clifton's turned out
some very very good riders. Great to see [Olympian] *Peter Smith*

Clifton Cycling Club, Horton in Ribblesdale 1960, Peter Burbidge on right (Peter Burbidge)

come to the club many years later and assist me and others in bringing youngsters along.

One day there'd been 20 of us out, we'd been to the Cow and Calf Rocks. My wife Rita was with us. We'd just got married. I was 23. She got tired, and she had the help of our ex-Lord Mayor Brian Watson. Although small of stature he was quite happy pushing my wife along. We came to the bottom of Poole Bank. You climb all the way up to the gates of the Harewood estate and you can turn off for Collingham, our teatime destination. I was getting fed up of my wife because she wasn't trying. She took one look at this climb and pulled back. She threw her bike that I'd built for her into the ditch bottom and wasn't going to move an inch for anyone. But then she got on that bike and flew

Ebor Cycling Club dinner 1961. Couple facing on right, Rita and Peter Burbidge
(Peter Burbidge)

up the bank and I'm watching her, thinking, "She'll never make
this hairpin bend. There can't be enough energy left in her". She
went round the hairpin bend so away I went up Harewood bank.
I still didn't catch her. She was sat with the rest of the cycling
club at Collingham having tea when I arrived. So the lesson is,
when your wife tells you she is absolutely tired out, don't believe
a word of it. The technique is getting that energy to work. She has
done some very hard runs with me, some colossal climbs.

As there were many youngsters interested, my aim was to take
out the junior section on good rides to Bolton Abbey and Grass-
ington. Some of these youngsters were only 14, I brought them
along, showed them the ways of cycling and techniques I'd
learnt over the years. My idea then was to let them go their own
way, once they'd got the experience, towards time trial racing, if
they wanted to go mountain bike racing which was just really
kicking off. I now see them, they're a group of young men with

families of their own. They just fly past me if they see me, "Get on your bike old man", is their usual call. Like the story of Mr Chips the schoolmaster, I've had so many of them in my years of cycling.

Cycling capes advert, 1954

Capes were very handy. If you had a tail wind coming home, we used to put our capes on and they acted like a spinnaker on a sailing boat, but they were very handy for other reasons. This particular day, we'd got up this country lane coming back from Spofforth. It had been a miserable day, raining. Some of the lads needed to make a stop. No cars flying around then. About four of them were stood, with the capes concealing their modesty. This lady popped out from nowhere with her two dogs and started talking to them. One was taking a bit longer than the rest of us. She says, "Well it's been a horrible day for you but it has dried up now hasn't it?" I said, "Not quite!".

You also have in York, the Wednesday Wheelers Rides, who are doing considerable mileage. It was to give people a chance to start cycling in retirement. You may in your prime be the club champion, but age starts to take over, maybe the odd illness and disability, a good club needs somewhere to bring young-sters into the sport, with room for them to develop and some of them perhaps ride the Olympics. What you need is continuity and a place for them that have been good in their day to have a toddle round and perhaps do 30 or 40 miles. The knockoff time is when you can no longer ride a bike.

I enjoyed every minute, the racing side, touring side, being a member of the club. The clubs wouldn't have managed without the mums and dads, who used to come and marshal the roads, putting out the marquees and getting everything set up. I loved it from 15 to 21. And I loved it in the early '60s but overall I've spent more time with the Clifton. The York rallies were nice days as well. I've had 60 years at it and it's all been very enjoyable.

One of the highlights of the York calendar is the annual Cyclists' Rally on the Knavesmire in June. Cyclists come from all over Britain and even further afield, and camp on the site for the weekend. There are demonstrations, family events and marquees with all the latest information for cyclists. There is also a parade through the city showing all kinds of bicycles. A more recent event in York is the annual World Naked Bike Race (held in 50 cities across the world) which attracts a hundred cyclists, bearing (!) the message *'Protesting against oil dependency: Celebrating bikes and bodies'*. The ride is actually clothing-optional and riders use body paint, flowers, feathers, flags and placards to spread the message.

— *Chapter 8* —

DIVING

Men's diving was first contested at the Olympic Games in 1904 and women's in 1920, though the first diving championship was organised in Scotland in 1889. Great Britain has never won gold medals, but has won two silver and four bronze.

York City Police swimming sports; PC Cutt, winner of Alderman Inglis cup for Plain Diving at Rowntree's Park swimming baths, 1920s (Northern Echo)

In York, diving has never been a significant sport though there have been swimmers who also dived. Initially, St George's swimming baths on St George's Field, Rowntree's Park baths (both demolished) and Yearsley baths near Rowntree's were used. In 1956 the York Coroner stated that the diving boards at St George's were dangerous and had to be removed. In more recent years, the Barbican had a diving pool, and St John's University had a pool with a high diving board, but both are now closed. Other clubs who used the pools were York City Police Club and York City Fire Brigade.

DENNIS WOODCOCK AND CYRIL JACKSON

Dennis Woodcock was well known in York for water polo and swimming. He was also a diver and won city competitions. He was regarded as the best diver in York when he was a teenager in the late 1940s. Cyril Jackson was a York swimmer and diver. At the Nunthorpe Grammar School sports held at Rowntree's baths in July 1933, it was reported in the local press that 'Cyril Jackson of the city swimming club gave a fine display of diving and swimming'. Dennis recalls

The highest board then was at Yearsley pool, about 15 foot high. You could do somersaults off the one metre springboard, one and a half somersaults, and do a back somersault off the top board. We [Cyril and Dennis] *put this show on at Rowntree's swimming pool. Cyril advertised for old fashioned swimming costumes with the sleeves in and legs, and we went round and collected about 15 of them.* [In the early years of the Olympic Games, diving participants were required to wear full swimsuits, 'cloth drawers at least six centimetres wide at the hip'].

We used to pretend that I was learning to dive. I would just flop in the water and he'd say, "No you do it like this". There was a box on the top of the diving board. He showed me how to dive off and said, "I'll save you if anything happens". I dived off and never came up, then I did come up and he swam over me, I came up again and he swam back over me, then up and down and up and down. Then I came up life-saving him. And that was the joke. In the Rowntree's magazine, there is a picture of me in a dress at the diving board, 'Dennis Woodcock clowning'.

Another time, Cyril would be doing a diving act off the boards and he told me to go round the side over the wall and give him some cheek as a little boy, with a school cap on, saying, "I can dive better than that". The pool was full of people and then he'd say, "I'm sick of you. If you can do any better, come round and do it. Shall he come round and show us what he can do?" So everybody shouts, "Yes", like a pantomime. I'd come round and the man who was on the door didn't know anything about it and he chased me right up the road, calling me a 'cheeky so-and-so'. In the end I had to tell him it was a joke.

Dennis Woodcock 1947, aged 14 (Dennis Woodcock)

I went in and came out in this frock, and Cyril did a jackknife off the board and everybody clapped and he says, "Now you go and do that". I says, "I can only do half a jack-knife". You know you touch both feet, I just touched one leg and then went in and the thing was blown then. We had loads of fun.

I once dived off the top board at St George's swimming baths. I was learning to do some dives for the Yorkshire competitions. I put my arms up to dive, brought them down, just ready to spring off, and unknown

*to me there were some soldiers racing to be first in the pool.
They changed, ran down the steps and dived in the pool. I was
in mid air and I hit this chap on his back as I was going in and
I went to the bottom of the pool not knowing anything about
it. Lonz [Webster, the baths superintendent] dived in and pulled
me to the top. I was about ten or eleven. I was taken to York
County Hospital and my dad came and picked me up and cross
barred me home on his bicycle.*

*Cyril used to be a Yorkshire diver, he was really good. Cyril and
I would give diving displays all over. He roped me in to dive off
Lendal Bridge in the Festival of Britain celebrations in 1951.
It was ten metres, which is 32 foot 6 inches, and I was used to
diving off 15 something foot. [I dived] off the board that they
hung off the railings, I was at the angle going into the water
wrong, and then carried over onto my back, and that really did
take the wind out of me. Some of the lads came to the cobbles
down the side and they talked me all the way back up, right
onto the bridge. "You're going to go again, because if you don't
go now, you'll never do it". So I went again in the right angle.*

*There was what you call plain diving, no somersaults. The
judges marked you for the entrance to the water, your flight,
putting your hands out. I did get to [represent] Yorkshire at a
pool in Leeds and I did get a win. In York, Frank Hardcastle
used to beat me, if anybody beat me.*

BROOKE MIDGELEY AND FRANK HARDCASTLE

Brooke Midgeley was part of York City Baths Club, in the days of
superintendent and manager, Lonz Webster. He recalls the diving
which took place at St George's Baths.

Lonz Webster was a character and a driving force. We didn't have time for socialising. We were training for an hour before work at seven, managed to fit half an hour in at lunchtime, and go to the club at half past six or seven until nine. We'd be there on Sunday mornings and Lonz would go to the golf club about eleven or twelvish so we'd have the place to ourselves. In the winter, the pool was absolutely overheated, we found if we opened the windows, we got this very thick fog. We'd be playing tig in this thick fog, there'd be lots of girls squeaking and blokes laughing, chasing each other all over the place.

One of the guys, Frankie Hardcastle, (he finished up as a pool attendant, he was involved in the closing down of St George's) got some ropes that they used for teaching people to swim, little harness on them, you towed them through the water, they were hanging down and he could get onto the top board of the diving boards, and there was a bridge over the rectangular pool. He could swing from one to the other and drop into the shallow end. Terry Boyes found that he could get up onto the heating pipes on the top and dive into the shallow end from a long way up. Then Lonz came back and caught us and frightened us to death. He banned us all for ages. When we were playing tig, Frank perfected this thing of jumping off the top board as close to the edge as you could so that you put your hands on the edge of the pool as you hit the water. So you jump straight out. As far as I remember, nobody got it wrong. You were within inches of jumping onto the concrete. We were crackers.

There was the old mortuary next door to St George's. Derek Stubbs worked at Shepherd's, so did his brother Donald, another swimmer. He built a trampoline shortly after the war in the old mortuary and Frankie Hardcastle used it for diving training. It was freezing in there, no heating. It wasn't anywhere you went for pleasure.

[The group went to heats in Blackpool] *and it was probably eleven o'clock at night, Frank was showing a group of us how to do a double somersault off the steps on the promenade into the sea. He found it was about six inches deep. Fortunately there was a lot of sand underneath it so he didn't damage himself. You needed nerve and commitment for diving. The 10 metre board at Derby Road baths, I went to the top of that, Terry Boyes had dived off so I was obliged to do it. I'd bought some new trunks for the national and they came off as I hit the water so I was swimming around underwater in the diving pit trying to find my trunks.*

Only Frank ever got to a national standard. He should have been on the stage. He could launch himself off the side of the pool, the water was only six or eight inches below the deck level and he could put himself into cross legs ... sort of 'reclining on a settee' attitude and then immediately turn it into a dive and go in neat from that height. He was a gymnast.

— Chapter 9 —
EQUESTRIANISM

Equestrianism was first contested in the Olympics in 1900, but only men in the military could compete until 1952. Britain's only gold medal has been Colonel Harry Llewellyn in 1952 on Foxhunter. The competition is divided into three sections – Dressage, Eventing and Jumping. Dressage is the performance part, (described as 'horse ballet'), which includes choreographed movement to music. Eventing involves an endurance test, and steeplechase. Jumping or Showjumping involves navigating an arena which has about a dozen varying fences. This is the only sport where men and women compete against each other equally.

York has a long history of horse racing but equestrianism is less popular, despite a number of riding schools in the area.

The Riding School and Club.

SCALE OF
CHARGES.

Private Lessons of 1
hour each :
Course of 12 Lessons
£3   0   0
Single Lesson ...   5   6
Riders wishing for more
than one hour should
apply to the principal.

Hunting.
Pupils wishing to hunt
should   enquire   about
special terms.

W. C. Marshall, Rawcliffe Lane, Clifton

The Riding School and Club advert 1928

FIONA MAYNARD

Fiona Maynard, from Stillington near York, began riding at the age of four. She got her first pony at 14. At the age of nine she was

Fiona Maynard (York Press)

diagnosed with Stargardt's disease which meant her sight began to deteriorate as a young teenager. She attended Bishop Burton College near Beverley. She has competed in able bodied dressage from elementary to advanced but mostly competes in para-equestrian dressage competitions as she only has 15 per cent sight. She is allowed to use the 'living letters' system where an assistant can call out letters as she approaches them in the arena. In 2010 she took part in the first inter-regional para-equestrian dressage competition. Her region, the northern squad, came second but Fiona was delighted to be the individual winning rider, riding 'United E'. She was first in the Grade IV Para class at Bishop Burton.

In November 2011 Fiona won a place on the British Equestrian Federation England Excel Talent programme where 50 riders with potential to represent their country in competitions, receive special coaching and top psychologists and physiotherapists. The riders come from dressage, eventing, showjumping and para-equestrian dressage disciplines and are encouraged to train making use of all the specialist help on offer and to develop their skills in a competitive environment.

Fiona also trains competition horses for amateur and professional riders.

— Chapter 10 —
FENCING

Fencing, one of the oldest Olympic sports, has been contested at each Games since 1896. In that year and in 1900, amateurs and professionals were allowed to compete for the only time. The French and Italians have dominated the game. In the 1924 Games in Paris, there was a dispute between France and Italy which resulted in a duel, though not one to the death! Gladys Davies, a British woman, won a silver medal in the foil event in 1924, the first time women had competed, and Britain's women also won medals in 1928 and 1932. The only British gold medal was won by Gillian Sheen in 1956.

The first mention of fencing in York, was in an advertisement in the *York Courant* of November 1781.

'Monsieur Paulie, who learned the art of dancing under the celebrated Monsieur Gardel, and fencing under Monsieur Juin (fencing master in the Royal Academy of Paris), purposes teaching those Branches of Education in this city, which he flatters himself he is perfectly capable of doing in the newest and best Taste, as now practised in Paris, and with the most Elegance and Precision. He has engaged Mr Nicholson's Great Room in Coney Street to accommodate the town in general and proposes keeping a Day-School and Evening School and will likewise be happy to attend ladies and gentlemen in their own houses'.

York Fencing Club was formed in April 1938, with headquarters at Manor School, Marygate. Its president was Anthony John of York Repertory Players, and the Hon. Secretary was M. Richmond Fox. They held a weekly meeting, open to both sexes, and by the end of the year, had 30 members. Matches were arranged with university and army clubs from various parts of the north of England. In February 1939 the club produced an 'assault at arms', involving a costume demonstration of medieval swordplay.

By 1961, fencing had become very popular in York, due to the commitment of Paddy Power. Membership of the York Blades Fencing Club was increasing and the club was appealing for any surplus masks, gloves, jackets and foils, and was prepared to 'make reasonable offers'. The secretary was Anthony Power, Paddy's son. Practice sessions were held on Tuesday and Friday evenings at Canon Lee School.

Today, the only fencing clubs in the city are those at the University of York, open to the public as well as staff and students, and a club run by Donald Walker at the Mount School.

PADDY POWER

Most sports people in the city are familiar with the name of Paddy (Patrick Francis) Power. He served with the Physical Training Corps at Fulford Infantry Barracks, and inspired young soldiers, receiving the MBE in 1945 for his services to sport in the military.

His son Anthony recalls,

My father was in charge of the Railway Institute during the war. He was a Regimental

Paddy Power *(Kate Cartwright)*

Sergeant Major and the Institute was the reception centre for all troops joining in the north part of England. Troops went through their basic training and did their physical induction at the Railway Institute. That was a really formative experience for him. Thousands of troops went through because it was the biggest sports facility in Britain.

Paddy became PT and fencing master at St Peter's School for 27 years and also an international fencing coach. He died in November 1977. In the Public Schools' Fencing Championship, there is a Paddy Power Cup for the highest number of points in the Junior section.

ANTHONY POWER

As early as 1964, Anthony Power was on the list of potential Olympic team members for the 1968 Games. In 1965 he was selected for the English foil team in the world championships in Paris, and represented Britain in the world student games in Tokyo in 1967, and the world fencing championships in 1969 and 1970. He won the British foil championships in April 1972 and went on to compete at the Olympic Games in Munich 1972.

I was born in York in 1945. My father taught fencing and boxing and swimming. He tried to get me interested in sport and reluctantly I did. The Fencing Club at the time used the historic buildings in York, Micklegate Bar and Monk Bar. It went with the ethos. Historical, swashbuckling. Small rooms but very atmospheric.

The club became quite well known in national circles. I became an international but there were quite a number of other people who preceded me onto that level from the York Fencing Club in the early '60s. It's all about luck and confidence and trying to go to the next level.

Anthony Power with national fencing coach Professor Anderson (Kate Cartwright)

It's changed a lot, in the sense that top sports people are now funded. For most international sports people, it has become a full time job. At that period, the rules on amateurism were very strict. If you took as much as a pound for a demonstration, you'd have been barred. It goes back to the Victorian period where you had the division between amateurs and professionals, gentlemen and players. Never the twain should meet.

Before the Olympics, Anthony was set to compete in the Commonwealth Games but was prevented by an accident whilst training.

The domesday scenario is when a blade breaks and enters your body. The blades are very flexible, but when they break it's like a broken bottle, it becomes a lethal weapon. When you have two fit guys coming at each other, very hard and fast, we approached each other at tremendous speed, his blade broke on my knee and ripped my leg open from knee to groin. I can still remember how it felt.

The clothing is stout, but you have to be able to move. So it's a compromise. Now there's a lot of carbon fibre woven in. In every sport there's the possibility for something disastrous to happen. You can have the equipment, you can have the rules, but at the end of the day something can go wrong.

For the Olympics, you qualify by competing in international events. Each round you get through, you accrue points and have to amass a certain number to be considered for selection. They pick the four with the highest number of points. I was national champion at that time. To reach that standard you need to train every day. Fencing and a lot of physical training, too. And that in addition to work is difficult to combine.

In any sport that has Olympic representation, it's the pinnacle. It's what everybody wants to do. In 2012 in London, everybody involved in sport would die to be there. It was the same for me, but I had decided that if I got there, that would be it. You invest so much time and effort and if you don't get selected, then it's another four years. Four years of that intensity is a long time.

My father and the fencing club supported me but it was expensive. You need a lot of equipment, it has to be of the first order. You're fighting with swords. The blades themselves don't last forever. There's foil, sabre and épée. You can do all three but you tend to specialise in one. I did foil which is light, fast, quite aggressive. You need probably six swords. You'd break at least one. Clearly you're up against people from France, Italy, Russia who technically were supremely gifted and it would be unlikely that you would reach that level of expertise. You can only use what resources you have. And being 6 foot 2 is a big resource.

In all sports, if you're left handed, it is an advantage.

You need a mask obviously to protect your face, a protective vest that stops the blade penetrating under your arm, a thick cotton jacket down to the wrist and up to the collar and then, because the scoring's now done electronically, a jacket that's got metal threads through it with a plastic lining. So you really are swaddled up.

Anthony Power *(Kate Cartwright)*

In those days it was the first to get five hits and there's a five minute time limit. One of the tactics is to put pressure on your opponent to make things happen. There's a lot of activity, it's very physically demanding. The average fight would last two or three minutes. You start off with 64 competitors and you're divided into groups of six and you fight everyone else in the six. And the top three go through.

Prior to 1936, judges stood behind and beside each fencer. In 1936, electronic scoring replaced the judges for the épée competitions. Before the 1930s, contests could last for several hours.

If you watch good quality fencing there's a tremendous amount of movement going on, not just with the blades but with the feet and the body. I did do six months of ballet as part of my training. I thought if I had that level of strength in my legs and that amount of control, I could only hope. It amused people tremendously, but I thought it was very good, I enjoyed it.

Anthony particularly enjoyed the world fencing championships in Havana in 1969.

That was my finest moment. I got to the semi finals. It was only because the weather conditions were so oppressive that other people kept falling over and couldn't stand the heat. I'd been training very hard so I was beating people that I would normally never have a chance of beating.

At Munich in foil there were four [competitors]*, and then four in the other weapons, and the women's team, so 16 in total. There's two competitions, an individual event and a team event where you fight everyone in the opposing team. I was selected for the team event. You travel there a week before, look at the facilities, get settled in, acclimatised. Foil is always first so you do your competition and then you support your team members and just enjoy yourself. I remember abortive attempts to make us march in a military fashion. We were drilled before the opening ceremony but you'll never get British people to march in step. Opening ceremonies are great occasions, you enter a stadium of 80,000 people of different countries, it was a great event.*

But the Munich games was marked by the slaughter of the Israeli team athletes. I still think that the games should have been abandoned. There were a lot of police around, and the news started to filter through and the Village was shut down. You were kept well away from things but it was a terrible event. I knew one of the Israeli athletes, a fencing coach, that was killed. I suppose it's changed sport forever. You're there to compete, possibly enjoy yourself, possibly do well, but it was the end of the road for those Israeli athletes.

There was security at Munich but it was lax. I went on to work for the Amateur Swimming Association and in the 1976 and

Fencing at St Peter's School (Kate Cartwright)

1980 Olympics the difference in security was quite marked. Much more checking and security, metal detectors, all the panic that you see at airports now, came in then.

We did okay, we won a few fights and I won my last fight against the reigning world champion. That's a nice departure point. My last bout at Munich was the last time I ever picked up a fencing weapon. I'd spent 12 or 13 years doing it and just didn't want to do it anymore. You'd put years and years of effort, to finally achieve the ultimate, that was a feeling of relief. And it's a good departure point, time to move on in life and do other things.

It had shaken the world, what happened in Munich. There were fears that it could be repeated in some way, somebody would try to hijack the event. Trying to provide security at major events is a nightmare. Moscow was a highly political Games, because the Russians had invaded Afghanistan two years before. There were calls for the British team not to compete. The Americans decided not to. The facilities were superb, the arrangements were good but the games were tarnished by some top teams not participating.

There was no drug testing at Munich. It came in 1976 and by 1980 there was a full regime. One of my jobs in Moscow was to accompany people to testing. They would be quarantined until they provided a sample, which can take some hours because they were seriously dehydrated. There were cases of swimmers [not in Britain] who were medicated without knowledge or coerced into taking drugs. The testing now is very rigorous. We talk about what's the purpose of sport. Is it about young people from different parts of the world meeting and enjoying one another's company? Is it about winning? Will people do anything to win?

Sport at international level has got nothing to do with coming together of nations. That's a myth that's put around, that it's to do with love and understanding. It's to do with competition. It's war by other means. When I was working for the Amateur Swimming Association I went to the world swimming championships in Berlin in 1978, held in the 1936 Olympic facilities, which is when everything changed in sport, when you saw sport used for other purposes than friendly competition. Since 1936 it's been about nationalism and countries trying to promote themselves. If you look at the bidding process, nations want to get that accolade. Japan was desperate to get that in 1964 because it was a rising nation that wanted to project itself onto the world stage. Russia in 1980 was desperate to achieve that recognition.

St Peter's Fencing team. Paddy Power in centre at back, Anthony Power on right at back
(*Kate Cartwright*)

But we have had very good success, given our amateurish approach to it. They always say there'll be a legacy and economic benefits but if you look back to what happened to most cities that have staged the Olympics, they've found it very costly.

After competing in the Olympics, Anthony went on to be a physiotherapist with the British swimming team and went to Montreal in 1976 and Moscow in 1980.

The national coach at that time was trying to professionalise swimming and realised that all the other swimming teams had support services – doctors, psychologists and physiotherapists. I was with them for some years, did world championships, Commonwealth Games, Olympics. It was a voluntary position. You'd go away three or four times a year. I was the only physio. Nowadays there's a whole team of people. You've got almost as many support staff as you have competitors. I think the important factor was to have that background in elite sport so that you were able to understand the stresses and strains that it generated. That sort of superhuman effort puts the body under tremendous stress. And at times it will go wrong.

People who win medals are a different breed of people. They've got to have the physical equipment, but I think it's more to do with their attitude, their belief that there's something different, extra special, about the gold medal winner. There is something indefinable about the quality they have that marks them out from other people. If you knew what it was, you'd bottle it and sell it.

Anthony went on to manage the new Priory Street Sports and Community Centre in 1979. The Centre was

quite a novel concept. York had always been well supplied with swimming pools, and at one time they provided quite a proportion of the British swimming team. But they've never been well provided for in public sports facilities. The 1970s was the era of the leisure centre. In York the Priory Street Centre was essentially run by the Council for Voluntary Service in the old school. Community sport as opposed to elite sport. It was a model for how you could get all sorts of people to try things. I've always been of a view that rather than having big elite sports facilities, you need a network of community facilities where young and older people can have an identity and feel comfortable.

If you can keep that friendly ethos of sport, I'm all in favour of it. Sport should be about enjoyment, participation, fitness, and at the elite end it's a different animal altogether. It's like comparing your family car to a formula one racing car. It's nice for us to look at wonderful elite performances and to try and do our best, but at the end of the day the important thing is to come away and say, "That was really good, I enjoyed that".

— *Chapter 11* —
FOOTBALL

Men's football as an Olympic sport began in 1900, but winning the FIFA World Cup, which started in 1930, has become more important than an Olympic title. England has only won the World Cup once, in 1966, but the Great Britain team won gold at the Olympic Games in 1900 (exhibition matches), 1908 and 1912.

York City football 1920s, Bert Keech is goalkeeper in middle at back (York Oral History Society)

Football has long been seen as the British national game, and York, in common with many other towns and cities, has a professional team, and a league of amateur clubs. It is a game that can be played at any level, by people with a lot of skill or very little. And the only equipment needed is a ball, although there was often improvisation. Andy Waudby who lived in Hungate in the 1930s, recalls,

We couldn't afford a ball. We went to the slaughterhouse and asked for a pig's bladder. We blew it up and played football. Or we made a parcel of old newspapers and used that.

Perhaps the first recorded mention of football in York is from the city's court records for 1565 which report proceedings *'against Christopher Dobson and Oswald Atkinson. That they have played at the football within this cathedral church of York. The football was brought into the Church by Dobson, and thereupon Oswald Atkinson did take the ball from him in Church, and there was but one stroke striken at the same in the Church'*. The boys were given an hour in the church stocks on the next Sunday morning followed by 'six strokes of the birch on the buttocks'.

York City team 1938 (York Oral History Society)

In 1897 the York and District Football League, one of the oldest amateur leagues in the country, was formed, with nine local clubs. Only Rowntree's has had an unbroken life since then. Over the years there have been clubs representing schools, colleges, youth clubs, working men's clubs, the railway, churches, pubs, army regiments, companies, both large and small, and local villages. The lists themselves almost form a potted history of York and it seems as if, at one time or other, every boy in York was playing the game. Most of the teams are long gone, such as the Scots Greys (based in York during the years before the First World War), the 5th Lancers, LNER Loco, Old Priory Adult School, York Gas Company, Malton Bible Class, Terry's Employees, Poppleton Sugar Factory, Armstrong Patent's and Naburn Hospital. Today the Leeper Hare Football League, (sponsored by Leeper Hare Developments), has more than fifty clubs, in premier, first, second and third divisions.

In 1900, the York City and District Football Association was founded and cup competitions launched. The first York City Football Club was established in 1908, with a ground on Holgate Road. A stand for 300 people was provided. The club went into liquidation in 1917, but, after the First World War, the Yorkshire League was formed for part time professionals. In 1922, the York City Football and Athletic Club came into being. A ground at Fulfordgate on Heslington Lane was bought for £2,000. But in 1932, a larger ground was required, and the official opening of the new ground at Bootham Crescent took place in August.

In the 1937-8 season the team reached the sixth round of the FA Cup, but its peak time was in 1955, when York City reached the semi final, despite being in the third division. In front of the biggest crowd they had ever faced, 65,000 at Sheffield, they drew with Newcastle United, 1-1, but at the replay a few days later, they lost 2-0. (Comparing figures of spectators at football matches shows how other forms of entertainment have overtaken the game in popularity. Today the average number at York City games is less than 3000). 1955 was the highlight of the club's cup runs, but the highest achievement was when they got into the second division from 1974 to 1976. For a comprehensive history of the club, see *'York City, a Complete Record 1922–1990'* by David Batters.

York City football ground 1955 (Mike Race)

An exciting moment for aspiring footballers in York was in April 1950 when the Daily Express advertised that footballing hero Stanley Matthews was to come to the Railway Institute to hold coaching sessions with free admission. About 2000 school boys turned up. Matthews picked out half a dozen and gave demonstrations of some of his skills.

STEVE MCCLAREN

The most internationally-famous York footballer is Steve McClaren who was born in the city in 1961 and attended Nunthorpe Grammar School, where he captained the football team. At 18 he began to play for Hull City, moving to Derby County six years later. He went on to play for Lincoln, Bristol and Oxford, before retiring through injury. Following a spell as assistant manager for Manchester United, he reached the heights in 2006 when he became England manager. His reign lasted less than two years and was not very successful, but in 2008 he moved to manage Twente, the Dutch side, and they were crowned champions for the first time in their history, in May 2010. Later that month, McClaren moved to manage a German team. In June 2011 he returned to England to manage Nottingham Forest but in January 2012 he moved again to manage Twente for a second time. At the first match, supporters wore t-shirts which read 'Welcome back Steve'.

ALF PATRICK

Alf Patrick, legend of York City Football Club, celebrated his 90th birthday in late 2011. He is the team's oldest surviving player and the only one to score five goals in one match, in November 1948, when he scored against Rotherham, with York winning 6-1. He was also the first man to reach 100 goals for York and is fourth on the goal scorers' list, with 117 goals from 241 matches.

During the war he served in the Royal Engineers' tank assault unit, so did not start his football career until he was 25. He was a part time professional, also working for Cooke, Troughton

Alf Patrick 1950s (York Oral History Society)

and Sims, and would train two nights a week. He was asked to join Sheffield United and West Ham, but decided to continue with York.

I was born in Layerthorpe in 1921 and played football for Manor School. Later I played for York City Boys, and then had a trial with Yorkshire Schoolboys.

There was a Daily Despatch competition all over the country, and we won the York area and the Yorkshire area, and then we played a team called St. Joseph's at St. Helen's for the final. We were winning 1-0, with two or three minutes to go, and one of their players kicked a long ball towards our goalkeeper and instead of trying to pick it up, he had an almighty lunge and it bounced back into the goal, so it was one apiece, so we held the cup six months each. That was in 1930. I played for Cooke's too, I was inside forward.

After the war Alf played with York City.

I played seven or eight games in the second team, then I got in the first team, centre forward. At Hull there were 42,000 there and we beat them 3-2. I was on the City ground for the cup run in 1938 against Huddersfield, there was 28,000 there. I started at about £2.10s [£2.50p] as a part time player. I used to go on a bike to the match, I'd think sometimes if I got a puncture I'd have been a bit late. You got two pound if you won, on top of your wages.

Alf stopped playing after getting a bad injury, but he'd had a number of previous ones.

In 1947, a real bad winter. I fell and broke my scaphoid bone [wrist]. Then I had me nose done once, and I used to have a bit of trouble with the hamstring. All they did in those days, you used to have like a sunlamp, and they'd put that on, laid on the bed. None of the fancy stuff that you get today. A magic sponge and a bucket of cold water. I had a plaster cast on my leg and when I got to bed I'd take it off. We lived in Penyghent Avenue, and when I'd finished with it I stuck it in our compost heap, there was this pot leg sticking up.

CHARLIE TWISSELL

Charlie Twissell has lived in York since 1958 but was actually born in Singapore in 1932. He is the only footballer in York who has played in the Olympic Games.

When I left school I joined the Navy and played football for the Combined Services. I was playing three games in a day at times. If you're in the forces and you're good at sport, you don't

England Olympic football team 1956, Charlie Twissell is 4th from right at back (Charlie Twissell)

107

do much else. I went to the Olympics in '56 in Melbourne. They just came up and said, "You've been selected to play". You didn't really work with the England team, apart from any matches that they might have fixed up. I played five internationals against other countries, Iceland, France, Wales, that was part of your selection.

We got knocked out by Bulgaria at Wembley. Some teams dropped out on political grounds and consequently they asked Great Britain if they could send a team out. We got through the next round but we didn't progress much further. We played a few matches on the way home, against the Singapore XI, we didn't stay for the rest of the Olympics.

There was a PT Instructor who recommended me when I came home, to two sides, Plymouth Argyle and Charlton. I signed with Plymouth Argyle.

The worst thing I did in my football career was to sign professional [in 1957]. Then it becomes a job. And I liked to play football. Once I got to that stage, the pressure was on, you had to do well because if you didn't, you got dropped.

In 1958, Charlie was transferred to York. He was paid £15 a week plus £3 for a win. He is remembered for a powerful kick in a game against Reading, launching the ball into the floodlights and smashing them.

I was a yard out of goal, I missed it and hit the floodlights. I thought I'd be arrested. I like those sort of things, it takes any pressure off.

York had a good team. A lot of local lads, Vic Wilkie, [Wilkinson], Mickey Grainger, Tommy Forgan, Peter Wragg, Georgie Howe, Barry Jackson, Barry and Peter Tate. They were

York City 1957, Charlie Twissell is second from right at front (Charlie Twissell)

a grand bunch. We used to do a lot of stamina training, lapping and running. As a footballer the football is your tool, you're finding out what you can do with it, what you can't do with it, how quickly you can do it. Tommy Lockie [manager from 1960–67] was a beggar for training. If you couldn't run for three or four hours at a time, you weren't fit. It was good because you knew where you were, you got on with it.

Charlie only played for York for three years but then decided to go back to amateur football. He helped to coach the Norton (near Malton) club.

I ended up working at Armstrong's and later in insurance. I played for the Wednesday half holiday league. It fitted in with my work and it was grand playing with some of the lads, and Guy Mitchell who had the sports shop.

109

The Olympics was an experience worth having. In amateur football you played because you wanted to. You weren't worried about, "If I play bad I'll be dropped next week", and if somebody nattered at you, you could say, "You haven't paid to watch this match so I'm answering you back". Today there's a lot more pressure. I don't know whether I could stand today's pace.

GUY MITCHELL

In 1976, Guy Mitchell, who had run Mitchell's sports shop in the city since 1950, started to sponsor the Mitchell Football League (mini soccer league), of local friendly fixtures. By the following season the league had 36 teams. (He also sponsored a cup for the York Vale Cricket League).

It was under 12s, some fathers had kids that wanted to play and the minor league didn't provide anything. The lowest age group was 14 to 16 but they were too young for that. They started playing friendlies, about eight clubs all run by parents. I was on the FA at the same time so I found them a trophy. Robson and Cooper did the engraving. Then they said, "Will you come on the committee?" I said, "You've first got to go to the FA and get affiliated". So we got the Mitchell League going. Then they said, "Will you sponsor it?" I really enjoyed that. Then we started an under 11s Ryedale league. The mini soccer league started about 1980. The present secretary, Barry Castleton, organises it all. It's quite complicated, all the fixtures for all different ages.

By 2005 there were 16 divisions playing mini soccer at nearly 30 clubs. The Football Association decreed in 2005 that under 7s should not play competitive football, and in 2008 this was extended to include under 8s.

— *Chapter 12* —
GYMNASTICS

Men's Artistic Gymnastics is one of the few sports to have been contested at every Olympics since 1896, though women had to wait until 1928. The sport consists of six sections – floor, horizontal bar, parallel bars, pommel horse, rings and vault. There are medal winners in each category plus ones for all-round performance.

There is also Rhythmic Gymnastics, only contested by women, using rope, hoop, ball, clubs and ribbons, and trampolining, which became an individual sport in 2000.

Rowntree's gymnastics demonstration, 1928 (York Oral History Society)

York Railway Institute gymnasium opened in 1926, offering boxing and gymnastics for adults. There were ladies and men's classes for the latter, and annual public displays took place in the city. After the Second World War, this continued, sometimes being called 'physical training'. The facilities were good, but interest in the sport began to wane as the 1960s dawned. Gymnastics at the Institute ended in 1979.

STAN WILD

Stan Wild was born in South Yorkshire in 1944, and he competed in two Olympic Games, at Mexico in 1968 and at Munich in 1972 when he was the oldest British participant at 28.

I started at school, a man called Bert Scales was my PE teacher and Bert became the national coach for trampolining. I didn't do any real gymnastics until I got to Carnegie College, [in Leeds] to train as a teacher. After a football match I walked past the gym and there's a lad practising some vaulting. He said, "I need someone to practise with, what about tomorrow night?" Tomorrow night became every night. A coach came to Carnegie with the national squad and I was invited to their training session. I became a regular competitor at British championships, representing them at floor and vaulting, and was North of England pole vaulting champion before I started gym, as a 15, 16 year old schoolboy. I was reserve for the European championship finals one year in Grenoble.

In 1918, there were women in Yorkshire who won medals. So we were good then, the two wars devastated the sport in this country. Originally it was called German gymnastics, after Ludwig Jahn, the man who used apparatus to train the military. In the 1920s and '30s, Germany wasn't too popular, and their gymnastics was forbidden. It became Olympic Gymnastics after 1964, and lost the German prefix. In the 1980s it became

Stan Wild on rings, Olympic Games 1968; chosen as Olympic torch bearer 2012 (Stan Wild)

Artistic Gymnastics. When I started, I probably knew everybody who did gymnastics in the country. Now I'll know, at the most, one per cent of the millions who participate. Now every school child wants to be a gymnast.

There are six apparatus. In the 1960s there were no specialists as there are now. We had to do all of them twice, a compulsory exercise on each and then three voluntary exercises. The floor exercises last up to a minute and a half, the beams a minute, the bars will take 30 seconds and the vault ten seconds. So a lot of training for a short time. It's a very explosive sport, very powerful. We would train two or three hours on the apparatus three or four times a week. In the 1960s and '70s I had to build my own apparatus, with a bit of help from one or two friends and my father, who got some welding done, and he got me some channel iron and things like that to make parallel bars. I made a pommel horse, set of parallel bars, a ring frame and managed to acquire a high bar and I put them out in my garden on the edge of a wood, and fastened my apparatus down to four local trees in the right place. And we trained on an evening with an outside light on the house, under the leaves which protected me if it rained. Mum and Dad bought me one

side of the parallel bars for Christmas and the other bar for my
birthday in February. And we trained on those every night when
I couldn't get to a proper gym.

Competing in two Olympic Games proved to be very different
experiences.

In 1968, [were] *trials to the Olympics and only two of us*
were selected to go to Mexico, a close friend, Mike Booth, and
I. Gymnastics was a bit of a Cinderella sport at that time. I
became team captain for the 1972 Olympics in Munich. We
managed to qualify a full team, six gymnasts.

At the Mexico Olympics the Mexicans were very happy-go-
lucky, 'Mañana', 'It'll be all right tomorrow'. Quite different to
the Munich Olympics which were a bit sombre and efficient.

Stan remembers the tragedy that befell the Israeli team at the 1972
Games.

We were about 100 yards away from the Israeli building. We
were woken up and told we were going for a bus ride to see
Ludwig's castle in Bavaria. We weren't very pleased. Then the
bus driver explained what might have happened. On the way
back to the village, we saw the helicopters flying over the build-
ings and at that time they'd taken people to the airport and
blown the aeroplanes up. Next morning we went down to the
Olympic stadium for a meeting with Avery Bundage who was
the president. He told us the games must go on. It was quite
traumatic at the time.

In 1969 Stan came to teach at St John's College in York.

My students were doing BEd degrees. I would have them once a

York Gymnastics Centre, Heworth (Stan Wild)

*week for three weeks, for an hour and a half gymnastics class.
At the time I left, there would be an hour's gymnastics for ten
weeks in their three year course. My reason for going there was
to improve the standard of gymnastics in the country, through
PE teachers. But there's no PE teacher training there now. I'd
go to school and take a club eight o'clock to nine, teach till
12.30 and have my dinner in the gym. Take a basketball club or
something and then, after school, football match, eat my tea
in the car and drive to Leeds or go home and do some training,
and collapse into bed. You have to be very dedicated to stick at
it because it wasn't easy. Everybody in gymnastics at that time
was passionate about it.*

*My first competition was Great Britain against Russia, acro-
batics and tumbling, and that cost £40 to go to Russia to
compete for Great Britain. The first month's wage as a teacher
was £39.17s so it cost me a month's wage.*

I competed for Great Britain for seven years, British champion for five, and did four world championships I think, '66 to '74, three European and two Olympics. I had a good run. In the 1970s the students asked me how to run a school gym club.

So he started a club at the college for local boys, and the students helped.

When the students left, children still wanted to keep coming and it became a gym club at the college. It enhanced the things we could offer. Some of the students went into York schools so they could stay and do gymnastics. The children kept coming so we started York City Gym Club. In 1972 Olga Korbut hit the Munich Olympics and the whole thing exploded. I used to get a phone call every five minutes to say, "My daughter's going to be the next Olga Korbut". So we introduced girls, and we started to get female PE students as well. We eventually had boys Tuesday

York Gymnastics Centre indoors, Heworth
(Stan Wild)

*and Thursday and girls Monday and Wednesday, then all of
them on a Sunday morning.*

York Gymnastics Club was officially formed in 1974, and began to run
an annual summer school in 1977, with championships and galas.

*Eventually we got to use Priory Street Sports Centre. We kitted
it out with all the things that were necessary to do Olympic
gymnastics. We had one of the first safety landing areas in the
country. A hole filled with foam cubes so they could somersault and land in the foam and go about four or five foot deep.
20,000 six by six by six foam cubes. By 1985 we had about 1000
members. I trained a lot of coaches and members of the public,
who came to help, and eventually built up the coaching staff.
About 1986 we were bulging at the seams. We decided we'd
fundraise and build our own.*

The Croft, in Heworth Green, part of the college, had a disused area at
the back used by dog walkers. The college agreed to this being used.

*So St John's bought the land. We were the sprat to catch the
mackerel so they could access this land. We moved all our
equipment out and brought it here. We designed it as big as we
possibly could because we knew what was likely to happen
once we started with our own facility and so for the last 25
years we've developed it into a gymnastics centre with a couple
of thousand members. We have 70 classes a week. I'm still
coaching, I'm still active.*

*These days people are aware of what dangers there are. All the
floors in this centre are sprung so there's no large impacts. We
have about twice as many girls as boys. We have trampolining
for both. We have mixed classes for that because they do the
same apparatus, whereas we separate them for the gym because*

they do different apparatus. Girls do floor vaults. They used to do rings and parallel bars but they were too physically strong for them, so they introduced the beam and the high and low bars, the asymmetric bars. The men still do the high bar, parallel bars, pommel horse and rings.

We run Yorkshire championships, we've had the England Girls' team here training for the weekend, and competitions with Soisson in France, and Ypres and Antwerp clubs.

Fortunately the college were generous and allowed us to build something worthwhile for the community. I couldn't underestimate how many thousands of people have been through this facility and benefited from it. More people come here in a year than watch York City Football Club. It's very developmental for the children. Increases the bone strength and density, keeps them fit, keeps them off the streets, stops them playing with drugs, so it's extremely valuable socially.

Chapter 13

HOCKEY

Men's field hockey is one of the oldest team sports in the Olympic Games, having been played since 1908 (apart from in 1912 and 1924), though women's hockey has only been contested since 1980. The English team got to the final in 1948 and won gold medals in 1908 and 1988, (when a York-born man, Richard Dodds, captained the team).

York has been a centre for many small hockey clubs over the years. In 1934, the programme for the annual York Civic and Gala Week, which included many sports displays in the city, mentioned that there were 20 hockey clubs in York, though by the end of the decade this had reduced to 15.

Corinthians hockey club c1936. Harry Murray 2nd right, Margaret Lyall 3rd left front.
(York Oral History Society)

The York Olympics Hockey Club was founded in 1948 by Yorkshire Insurance Company as a mixed team. It was based in Acomb and moved in 1967 to the Railway Institute ground at New Lane. It split into men's and women's sections but the men's section disbanded in 1958. At that time York had seven hockey clubs – York Hockey Club (founded in the 1890s), York II, York Olympics, Rowntree's, Terry's, the Railway Institute and the York Trojans (founded in the 1920s). The Civil Service had its own club and ground at Boroughbridge Road. One York supporter recalls travelling with the team to a tournament in Blackpool in 1955, and that the players wore bowler hats all the time, (except on the field!) as a 'badge of office'.

In 1956, the York Olympics women's section won the 22nd Yorkshire Women's Hockey Association rally on Knavesmire, where 60 teams played 175 matches on 15 pitches. The club celebrated its silver jubilee in 1973 by winning the annual rally again, being the only unbeaten team from more than 60 competitors.

Terry's ladies hockey team 1960s (York Oral History Society)

Acomb Hockey Club was formed in 1968 with the amalgamation of the former Phoenix Hockey Club and York Spartans. It became part of Acomb Sports Club, situated behind Acomb Green, sharing the home ground and clubhouse with Acomb Cricket Club, but also has a pitch at Energise on Beckfield Lane.

York Hockey Club and York Trojans merged in 1998 to form the City of York Hockey Club, based in Heworth. They were joined by York Ladies Hockey Club in 2001. In 2006, the club became the first in North Yorkshire to receive England Hockey's ClubsFirst award. The following year the club merged with the University of St John Hockey Club. York University also has its own hockey club.

DEREK BELLERBY

Derek Bellerby, a member of the well-known York family firm of painters and decorators, died in early 2012. He was born in York 1923 and attended Bootham School. His father played hockey

for Yorkshire once and was on his way to play twice, which would have probably given him a cap, but it was cancelled. We played at Bootham, and had Stanley Elliott, who played for Yorkshire, as a master. He was only too keen to get it cracking. We had a First and Second XI.

As well as playing for the school,

I joined York Hockey Club in 1939. I was right wing. We didn't have a ground. We played all over. My first stick cost 18/6d. There was more timber in that stick than the latest ones. [Wooden sticks have now been replaced by materials such as aluminium or carbon fibre ones]. *They've got nothing about them at all. You can pay up to £200 for a stick. The club didn't really have any pads for the goalkeepers because they were very expensive.*

England hockey team 1956, Derek Bellerby second from right, front row (Derek Bellerby)

I had to be really careful with the shin guards because I had a bad leg from an incident at rugby at prep school. I was told I would be lucky if I could walk again. Of course at that age you ignore that, I wanted to run, so I ran. I didn't want to get it hit. So I went to a saddle shop and got the bit they put under the saddle and made a shin guard out of that.

During the war you found it difficult to get teams to play against. We used to play RAF sides often. We went once and were met by a very nice lady officer and suddenly the penny dropped, they'd got us to go and play against a ladies' side. So we split up and played mixed hockey and we had a meal and a bit of a dance and it was wonderful. When we played away, we'd go in cars. One had to be very careful because they paid half a crown to the driver for petrol, and of course by doing that, we were against the insurance. Then when the petrol was rationed, we went by train or by bus. It was rather nice because we were all together then. You got third class return fare and the hotel. You always had a dinner afterwards.

We were given the ground at Elm Park by Kaye Brothers. They couldn't get permission to build on the land so they gave it to the Hockey Club. Raylor's gave us their office, a Portakabin type thing and we moved it from their place to be our pavilion.

We had a pavilion built [in the 1960s], *but funnily enough it wasn't as nice an atmosphere as we had in the Raylor's ex office. It seemed to be so friendly, just something about it.*

Derek was then chosen to play for Yorkshire and then the North.

I played for 14 years for the county, got picked for the North, the best result was beating the South, the first time for over 40 years. I managed to get a captaincy of the North as well as the captain of Yorkshire.

I didn't mess about with the captaincy. Occasionally we had an RAF fellow from the South who came up. He was a very good player but he'd sometimes stop, just didn't do anything. At half time, I said to him, "I hope you're with us in this next half. So far you haven't turned up. I want a bit more". I went off to my wing and he was a bit annoyed. He ran straight through and scored. He looked at me and I said, "What about another one?", and he laughed and we were great friends. You have to lead by example. I wasn't aggressive in the wrong sense. We'd play against Cheshire and they always played, in my opinion, better hockey than we did, but we used to beat them. I always said that flair is some- thing you can't teach people, it was in them or not. The main thing is to be able to assess the situation on the field at all times. Today they don't have to worry what the pitch is like because they're all the same, easy to play on. They don't reckon on two fellows that might be marking them at different times, how fast they are and whether they're good or weak on the reverse side. That is what you've got to learn very quickly. If you had a blue from Oxford or Cambridge you had a very good chance of getting on. I played against two fellows with blues that I didn't reckon were as good as they thought they were. There were some very good players, don't get me wrong. Some of them remarkable, but they thought we were cloth caps and whippets.

Two other members of York Hockey Club played in the county side, P Rickets and Alan Dodds who was French master at St Peter's. His son Richard Allan Dodds played hockey for England. His team won a bronze medal at the 1984 Los Angeles Olympics, and he was captain, at the age of 29, of the gold medal winning Great Britain team at the 1988 Seoul Olympics. Although born in York, he was brought up in London where he attended Kingston Grammar School, and he went on to Cambridge. Now a consultant orthopaedic surgeon, he won 79 caps for England and was awarded the OBE for services to hockey. Derek was nicknamed Streaky because he ran so fast. He was selected to play for the England team against Wales in Guildford in March 1956. He also played for the England B team, for the second time, against Holland in Folkestone, at the end of the same month.

And 20,000 came to watch. I was very lucky. I'd been bypassed several times and missed it. It came out of the blue when I was 34.

It was his first international cap though he had played in two international trials. He was the fourth York player to represent England. The others were Sir Haviland Hiley, founder of York Hockey Club, and general manager of New Zealand Railways during the First World War, J L Wood and Kenneth Chilman. Derek remembers Chilman as

master at St Olave's. He used to cycle down to Bellerby's in

Petergate to congratulate me when I made a move up, and wish me all the best. Coming from a chap who was getting on a bit, on his cycle there, that played 21 times for England, I thought that was lovely.

The first thing I did when I went anywhere was to find a decent club and put my name forward to get a trial and hope that I'd be accepted. And immediately you had friends. I played for Blackburn which I enjoyed very much, played and umpired in Blackpool. It was great fun.

In later years Derek was a chief coach for the North, and he stressed the importance of team work. He then became

a selector for Yorkshire for a time. They were a fairly old set of fellows. Some had played a very high standard. I managed to get one thing clear. I said, "I know I've not been a selector for more than two matches, but I think we're wrong in selecting a fellow to play for the county, and if he doesn't play too well, get rid of him. Wouldn't it be better to give him two games, so if he's got nerves to start with, he isn't obliterated first time and never gets another chance?" They thought it was a good idea and it was put into practice.

Derek's sons Julian and Marcus also played hockey. There was

Only one occasion when I played with both of them at Bootham Old Boys and was carried off to hospital. I wasn't playing in glasses and my sight wasn't as good as it should have been. I caught the turf with my stick, hit my stomach and went over and damaged a rib. So I had to go to hospital. That's all they saw me play.

Derek and his wife also enjoyed the social side of hockey.

*We used to play on the Saturday and then again on Sunday
after the dinner and dance. We had some great friendships. I
was fortunate enough to get six of our friends* [hockey players]
*that I've known for over 50 years and I take them each year in
November for a long weekend and we call ourselves the Last of
the Summer Wine. It's important to keep going.*

ANN ROBINSON (NÉE BOUGH)

*Left: Ann Bough, South African tour 1969; Right, Ann Robinson née Bough, First team
York Women City of York Ladies hockey 1963–4 to 2003–4. (The Press)*

Ann Robinson (known to her team-mates as Robbo) was educated at
York College for Girls and joined York Women's Hockey Club (now
City of York Ladies) in 1962, captaining them to three Yorkshire cup
wins. She first represented North Wales in 1968 (because of her Welsh-
born father), and the North of England in 1970. In 1969 she toured
South Africa and in 1973 the West Indies, with the Welsh team. Ann
gained eight caps for Wales. She was selected for the Yorkshire County
team, captaining them for two seasons, in the late 1970s.

— *Chapter 14* —

JUDO

Although judo originated in 1882 in Japan, it only became an Olympic sport in the 1964 Games in Tokyo. There are seven categories, from heavyweight which is 100kg and over, to extra lightweight which is 60 kg, for men, and heavyweight of 78 kg and over, to extra lightweight at 48 kg for women.

In 1953, the York Railway Institute formed a judo club. By the late 1960s it had one of the largest competitive areas in the country. It was one of the first group of clubs in the UK to achieve a Sport England Bronze Clubmark.

York Railway Institute Judo Club, 2003, club golden jubilee, Neil Adams Olympic silver medallist with Jamie Bunyan on top (York Railway Institute Judo Club)

JOHN BUNYAN

Judo had started unofficially before this time, as John Bunyan, Chairman of the Railway Institute and treasurer of its judo club, explains,

There was judo at the Railway Institute just after the war, mainly with servicemen coming back, that knew how to practise it. It wasn't registered as a British Judo Association club until 1953. It had got to a point when there was the need for the coaching to be formalised.

[The dojo, or judo hall in the gymnasium] *came upstairs at the Institute when the boxing section folded. We've got permanent mats. Most clubs in Yorkshire and Humberside don't have the luxury of permanent mats.*

The club has what they call a club mark, which is a charter, it says you're a child friendly organisation. You have all the checks in place. It's good practice. It takes a bit of effort to get it, a bit of commitment from the coaches, and none of the coaches get paid. They all do it for the love of what they do.

We do training two nights a week. The youngest we take them is eight years old. It is a contact sport and people can get hurt so it is quite strict in the way that they are coached. The behaviour part is very important. They can't afford to have two or three unruly ones running around. It isn't about fighting. It's more about self control. And there is a lot to learn, a lot of complicated throws, and everything's in Japanese.

Although John is on the committee, he does not take part himself.

I started here because my two sons came to do judo. They went to college, came back to York and carried on. I've been involved

since my eldest son was nine years old. He's now 40, he's a senior coach. We have seven coaches. [Jamie Bunyan is a 4th Dan and his wife Bev is 5th Dan, they are both senior examiners]. *This was a railway club and to manage the facility you had to be an employee on the railway. That has all changed. The Railway Institute is open access. But I worked for the railway. I'm also involved in activities in the gymnasium and at New Lane ground.*

Densign White (Commonwealth Games gold medallist) & Elvis Gordon (who took part in three Olympics and sadly died in 2011), visit York Railway Institute Judo Club, with 2 girl members c1980 (York Railway Institute Judo Club)

To do judo you need to belong to a club. To grade, to change the colour of your belt, and progress in the sport through the national governing body, you need a membership licence. Every time you do a grading, change the colour of your belt, or learn the next step, there's a cost. You have national guidelines, a structure for grading that goes from a complete novice up to a black belt, up to a Dan grade. A child's gee [uniform] costs about £15, in comparison with a football shirt, it's nothing, but you can pay £150.

We always have two coaches on a mat. The first group will be complete beginners, 8 and 9 year olds. We try to keep them physically all about the same build. The next group is the young teenagers, 11 to 13. The hardest bit for them is the transition when they get to 16, to seniors. We tend to lose a lot of players because it's a difficult step to start practising with men. They always have a white belt, then when they join the Judo Association, they send them a red belt. So everybody that has a red belt

York Railway Institute judo coaches - Phil Jay, Jamie Bunyan, Simon Hill, Beverley Bunyan 2003, club's jubilee (York Railway Institute Judo Club)

has a licence. They've got three stripes, three level gradings, they just learn simple terminology and the basics. Then the fourth stripe, it goes to a yellow, three more it goes to orange, and then to green, blue, brown, then black, Dan grade. Very few children get a Dan grade. You really have to have the strength and ability to compete with men. It's all done on weight.

There is also discipline about the uniform, and members are expected to keep it clean and have a shower before the class starts.

And we don't like them out in the street in their judo suits. We live in a world where it could become a point of conflict. They're coming onto the mat and we try and keep that clean. People do get infections. It's just good practice.

The man who developed judo in its modern form, Kano, took it from the old Japanese martial arts. He formalised it like a PE keep fit regime in schools and universities. The majority of people do it for the exercise and learning the skill. The club's got about 80 members, of which between 50 and 60 are juniors. Competition isn't the main element at this club. There are clubs around the country where they compete for everything. We don't here.

There are fewer girls in the club,

Which is a shame, because girls tend to be more coordinated than boys. If they stick at it, they tend to be better at it. You don't need physical strength, you just need commitment and technique.

The club has been successful in its exchanges with other clubs. In 1977, for example, the senior men's team beat a visiting team from France, with a squad of 20 competitors. During the 1970s and '80s they won many titles at the Yorkshire team championships. In March 1980 at the county men's individual championships, the senior team won three gold, three silver and a bronze medal. One of the gold medals was won by Dermot Heslop, who was aged 19.

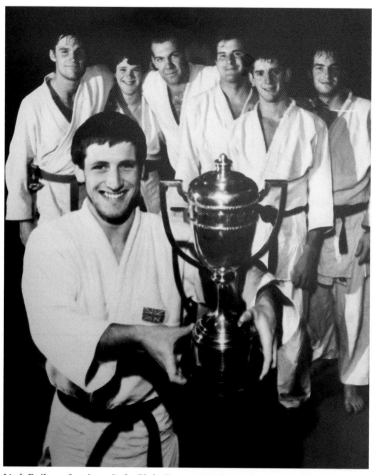

York Railway Institute Judo Club, Dermot Heslop at front, captain with York-shire and Humberside senior men's club championship trophy 1980s. Others L to R - Jim Ferguson, Adam Smith, Nick Gale, Chris Chadwick, Robert Reed and Mark Shepherd (York Railway Institute Judo Club)

DERMOT HESLOP

Dermot started out at the club in the 1960s, gaining his black belt in 1979, and his 6th Dan in 2004. He was captain of the club's A Team in 1984, a member of the British squad from 1979 to 1984, and became a British champion and international player. He won medals at various championships including trials for the 1980 Olympics. He moved on to be a coach and examiner, was national coach for Northern Ireland and National Development Officer for the British Judo Association and Sport England, and is now National Schools Development Manager. He still has connections with the RI club, and is honorary president.

ROB THOMAS

York man, Rob Thomas, was British number one judo heavyweight for some years. At the World Masters Judo Championships in Vienna in 2004, he was fifth in the 35-39 year age group and first in his category in the 2005 World Championships in Canada. In 2007 he announced that he was not going any further, believing that the problem in England is the lack of international standard facilities compared to other countries, and that the lack of funding was holding back some of those sportsmen and women who were good enough for the Olympics.

— *Chapter 15* —
ROWING

Rowing has been contested at the Olympic Games since 1900, though only since 1976 for women. Britain is second only to the USA in Olympic medals, with a record of 54 (24 of them gold), and in the years since 1900, there were only five Olympics when Britain did not win a medal. It is the only sport where Britain has won gold at every Games since 1984. Steve Redgrave is the only rower to win gold medals in five straight years, followed by Matthew Pinsent who won four golds. York has a long history of rowing. The White Rose Rowing Club held its first informal regatta in 1843, and the first official one in 1865. The York Amateur Rowing Club was founded in 1866. In 1905 the two clubs amalgamated to form York City Rowing Club. The club was all-male until women were accepted as full members in 1961. In 1909 the club bought land and a boathouse near Scarborough Bridge, at the end of Sycamore Terrace.

Rowers on Ouse for York Civic Week 1928. (York Oral History Society)

The club now has a membership of over 200, and holds five main events each year. It also sends crews to national events, and in 2007 a crew won at Henley. There are three other clubs in York, St Peter's School, York St John University and York University.

The hardest time for the club was when its wooden boathouse was set on fire by local troublemakers in 1954. Only one boat was saved. A new boathouse was built the following year, extensions were added, and a new clubroom and bar built in 1973. To tie in with the city's 1900th celebrations in 1972, a new boat was named 'York 1900'. Amongst many achievements, the club made history by reaching the last 16 of the Thames Challenge Cup. In March 2012, it was awarded lottery funding of nearly £30,000 towards refurbishment of the boathouse.

ALLAN WHITWELL

Allan Whitwell is the only York-born rower to compete in the Olympics. Born in 1954, he first went to York City Rowing Club when

I was about 11. It was my uncle's suggestion. He was an ex-rower from the navy. My uncle encouraged my brother to go, and within six months, they needed a coxswain, so I was dragged down. I went to Acomb Secondary School.

We went down [to the club] *all the time, a group of us under Baz Turner. Wilf Mellor was also involved, keeping a watchful eye on us. It was much more relaxed than it is now. If the adults had finished with them, rather than get the boats into the boat-house, we'd take them out for a little scull. We learnt by falling in and teaching ourselves a bit of watermanship.*

I left school and got a job at British Sugar Corporation on Boroughbridge Road. Paul Childs, the accountant, was a member of the rowing club. As I progressed through as a 16, 17

year old, doing more
sculling, he was
keeping an eye out
for me. Then British
Sugar arranged a
job in Tower Hill in
the sales office so I
could train and have
a chance to make
the Olympic team in
late '75.

Rowing has always
been an elitist, public
school sport.

Allan Whitwell, school boy at York City Rowing Club,
novice four, with Division Y trophy 1970 (Allan Whitwell)

It was very much Leander, [prestigious Henley rowing club],
Oxford and Cambridge guys. Even in the '60s and '70s it was a
bit of a class clash.

To keep up with the coaching and work that was needed, Allan moved
to London and then to

Nottingham in the early '80s. They pride themselves with all
the facilities they've got, ice rinks and the national watersports
centre.

In York, there's a lot of energy in the rowing club, a lot of will-
ingness to help people along. I was working shifts at British
Sugar, so in the afternoon after I'd slept, it allowed me to train
perhaps more than most, because of limitations of being on the
water in the dark. I was doing two or three hours training a
day. I just enjoyed it, the release of a young man's energy.

Baz Turner was very influential, he dragged me out once even though I'd got a hangover, he said, "Get out and row". He certainly toughened us up. Rowing has become one of the top sports, they've got Dorney [Eton rowing centre] *and Caversham* [in Reading, which has the Redgrave Pinsent Rowing Lake]. *So the whole structure's there with all the lottery funding. We were very much the last of the non-sponsored athletes. It was a big sacrifice. I sold my car so I could buy a boat to race in. Towards the end we were helped, once we'd won the lightweight world championships. After the Olympics in '76, I went to college* [and became a teacher].

Allan Whitwell with Paul Chiles by river, York City Rowing Club (Allan Whitwell)

In honour of
The British Team at the Olympic Games
The Prime Minister
and Mrs James Callaghan
request the honour of the company of

Mr. Allan Whitwell

at a Reception at the Banqueting House, Whitehall, S.W.1
on Wednesday, 1st September, 1976, from 6.00 p.m. to 8.00 p.m.

An answer is requested to
The Secretary (Invitations),
10 Downing Street, Whitehall

Invitation to Allan Whitwell from 10 Downing Street (1976 Olympics) (Allan Whitwell)

If you're a blue boat man, Oxford or Cambridge, you get imme-diate Leander membership, the great and the good around there get the membership initially. When I started to go to southern regattas, people were a bit shocked that I could actually beat some of the guys. It wasn't the norm for somebody from York to be brought into the GB squad. I had a very good coach, Ron Bircher, who took me under his wing for a couple of years and that helped enormously in the technical side of the sport. There wasn't much of a chance to stay in York. The coaches would have helped to move you on, but you needed the quality of athletes to be pushed against.

If you're good enough on merit, it doesn't matter what colour blazer [you have]. *I coach some athletes now and we have an issue with selection policy, because someone from Leeds is not getting the breaks that some of the others, from more estab-lished clubs, get.*

Allan has competed as a single sculler, in pairs, quadruples and eights. He was heavyweight winner at the Mannheim International Regatta in 1982, and a Diamonds finalist at Henley Royal Regatta the same year. He went to three Olympic Games, Montreal, Moscow and Los Angeles, winning silver at Moscow in 1980.

I came back to York after the Montreal Olympics for four or five months. Tony Power [Olympic fencer] *helped me enormously with body and strength conditioning. Part of the fun in 1976, we didn't have a lot of money. We were scrimping and saving, we had to varnish our own boat, just make do with what we had.*

I didn't go back in an eight until 1980. We were only together for 100 days. [The crew had never rowed together before the Olympic trials]. *The boat itself wasn't prepared for the Olympics, so to get the medal at the end was quite incredible. I was up in the bow. I was on the small side to race against the really big guys.*

Olympic silver medal crew 1980. L to R - Duncan McDougall, Allan Whitwell, Henry Clay, Chris Mahoney, Andrew Justice, John Pritchard, Malcolm McGowan (out of picture Richard Stanhope, Colin, now Lord Moynihan –cox (Allan Whitwell)

Allan Whitwell on left with Carl Smith, World Championships 1986, winning double sculls. Coach Ray Sims, who built the boat, in centre. (Allan Whitwell)

Allan's cox in the 1980 Olympic crew was Colin, Lord Moynihan. During the race, when the steering cables broke, he had to grab the rudder to steer the boat. Lord Moynihan was Shadow Minister for Sport from 2003–5. He then became Chairman of the British Olympic Association for the run up to the 2012 Games.

I'm one of only five men in the world, (there'll be some women), that have won heavyweight events and lightweight events. I was able to do both in '86, '87. I finished off my career in light-weight.

Allan now has an international sculling camp in France.

It's a nice way of life and I meet some really good people. I came out of teaching for a time when I was doing some profes-sional rowing for the British and the Norwegian teams. [He was chief coach for the Norwegian team in 1993]. *There is still great*

*camaraderie for people. There are friendships that are made
through the sport.*

The World Championship in Nottingham in 1986 was Allan's highlight, when he won the Lightweight Double Sculls with Carl Smith,

because the world championship was a win, and the silver [in
Moscow], *somebody beat us.*

Winning was

*Like an out of body experience. Almost like bursting a bubble.
Other people buoy you up. You don't understand the importance
of it until later. But other people have shared that moment.*

BRIAN SNELSON

Brian Snelson, current Treasurer for York City Rowing Club, came to
York

*in 1960 and joined the rowing club the second day I was here,
having rowed at university. I've been a member for just over
50 years. When the boathouse burnt down in 1954, they built a
new one on West Esplanade next to the war memorial garden.
In the '60s we put in a gymnasium floor and then in the 1990s an
extension was added.*

*I've seen the quality of rowing grow in York and that's mainly
due to the people we have coaching. They've done a tremendous
job. We're the only rowing club in North Yorkshire that can
offer rowing to people not at a public school. We've got a very
successful junior squad, up to international level. For the last
three years, York has won more trophies than any other club
in the country. There was very little rowing during the Second*

York Regatta Challenge Cup Crew 1910. C Clifford, bow, J A Little, T Batty, A B Dodds,
stroke, A E Holmes at front (cox). (Michael Saville & Brian Snelson)

World War. It started again in 1946. In the 1947 flood, the old
boathouse started to lift and float away. They tied it to a telegraph pole which is still there. When the wooden structure burnt
down in 1954, the land was then leased to the council to provide
school rowing. So York Education Committee had it rebuilt
and managed to acquire a few boats. Archbishop Holgate's
Grammar School rowed quite successfully until they lost their
sixth form.

When I rowed, there was one eight, six fours and six sculls.
No pairs or doubles. Now we've got a full range, probably 100
boats. The regatta season lasts from about the end of April.
Between October and March we start racing in timed races
called the 'Head of the River', the culmination being the London
one, usually the week before the Boat Race, and over the same

course, but the other way, between Chiswick and Putney Bridge. All the times are computered up and we find out who is the fastest. The one in York is on the third Sunday in November.

Last November the race still went ahead despite thick fog.

It was touch and go as to whether we would run it. We had 420 crews entered and 389 actually raced from Fulford up to King's Staith. We call it the 'York Small Boats Head', just singles, pairs and fours. When it floods we have to cancel. We lost it two years ago. It was about a metre and a half up. Apart from trying to marshal that number of crews on a fast moving river, we can't get them onto the water on time.

The women's section is expanding. There is

A ratio of three men to two women. Rowing in York is done on a status basis. You start off as a novice. You are able to race

York City Rowing Club At Home 1912 (Michael Saville & Brian Snelson)

other novices. The minute you've won something, you gain a point, then depending on how many points you can put together in a crew, will depend whether you race at intermediate or senior level, meeting people of roughly your standard. It's still heavily influenced by the public schools, because they've got the equipment, the coaches, and quite often the river to do it on. But it's certainly changed.

York City Rowing Club 1913 (Michael Saville & Brian Snelson)

We'd normally expect to pay £300 for an oar. We just bought a set for £2000, and that was a deal. They are made from special carbon, not wooden anymore, now high tensile. The boats we used to row in, you'd made the grade if you were allowed to get into one of the shiny smooth sculled thin-skinned fine craft. Before that you had to row in the clinker built ones. Now everything's fibre glass or plastic, which means if you get a hole in it, it has to go back for specialist repair. Everything we do in the club is entirely voluntary. We've usually been fortunate in having a few engineers or craftsmen in our members.

All the coaches are volunteers, it's an even bigger commitment because some of the best coaches are still racing themselves competitively. So somebody who's in the crew training hard for Henley Royal Regatta, is also being asked to lend a hand with juniors or novices. They do their training and then some coaching, then next thing you find them washing the boathouse out.

Henley Royal Regatta is usually at the end of Wimbledon. We have to qualify, either have a crew which is seen to have won quite a few prestigious events through the earlier part of the season, or go down and qualify.

The juniors do four afternoons a week training plus the Saturday. It's not for the faint hearted. It's for the dedicated, those that want to really row. You've got 60 juniors and there's competition for places, which is a healthy situation. You have to be able to swim the length of the swimming bath in your

N. Law's Eight on Ouse with old York City Rowing Club boathouse in background
(Michael Saville & Brian Snelson)

York City Rowing Club Regatta 1914 (Michael Saville & Brian Snelson)

rowing kit. The gym training is pretty scientific. Rowing was one of the first sports that really took it on and built on things that Roger Bannister had done in the 1950s in terms of cardio-vascular endurance, and building the strength up. You can see the difference now, the things they can do make me feel ancient.

We elect new captains the first Sunday in September. They're straight into it. Most of the people we recruit have just left school or university. The advent of the rowing machine has made quite a difference to training. It doesn't rock about, but the feel of it is pretty good. You can teach people a lot of the technique without getting into a boat. You're measuring the person on the machine, you can see his speeds on the display. The captains write down the score and they will expect to see an improvement.

The club also runs 'learn to row' courses

in May, when the nights get light. They last about six weeks.

The big disadvantage of the Ouse is the way that it goes up and down. It's the second busiest river in England, with pleasure craft and a huge marina at Naburn which didn't exist in our day. We could get down to Naburn without seeing anybody once upon a time, even on a summer afternoon. In winter, it [the river] *goes up four metres from summer level. There have to be high banks. It makes it more difficult to get at the water. The emergency services have had to mark certain points and reference them on their plans. It is quite horrendous sometimes, trying to race among the river traffic. There are safety launches out and monitoring boats. Not long ago we could run the 'Small Boats Head of the River race' and just let them go where they want.*

MICHAEL SAVILLE

Michael Saville is the current president of the club, though he

started rowing at St Peter's, in the Manor House. We'd have house races in the Easter term. In the summer term we went into competitive rowing, and I made my way up to the first four and the first eight, and got my school colours. We had a rowing master, Tudor Howat. He'd take us out in clinker boats, fairly crude ones. He taught me the fundamentals of rowing, it was through him that I entered regattas.

I left school in '54 and went to London. I rowed with Quintin Boat Club. That's where the Oxford crew comes in after the boat race. I went down there as a senior oarsman. But I realised there was a tremendous difference between the standard of rowing in the north and the south. Everything was hinged around Henley, but it's very different now. I got my opportunity to learn how to row on the tideway and get to a higher standard. Then I came back to York. In 1960 I was on the general committee, I was captain of the club. My father was an oarsman and he was president of the club.

We just didn't have the equipment then, we couldn't afford it. When we entered one of the first 'Head of the River' races, we were rowing with blades which were rather narrow. Suddenly everybody was talking about spade blades. The surface area was twice as great, so you could make the boat go much faster. We bought a second hand set for £75. Of 400 crews, we came 45th. That was the highest that anybody had been from our

York City Rowing Club c1958; Mike Saville back row, 4th from left.

(Michael Saville & Brian Snelson)

club. That was eight people who had a real commitment and all thought the same, trained hard, spent a lot of time on the river.

It gave me enormous pleasure to see a northern club getting well up the ladder in the results. We're fortunate in having one of the finest rivers. You can row from Naburn Lock up to Linton without any restriction at all, about 20 miles, which is most unusual. Some clubs, if they manage to get two or three miles, that's the extent of their rowing.

The number of children who are members is increasing.

Mothers bring them after school, even driving in from Pocklington, or Wakefield, and four days a week they will row. That's the level of commitment. We couldn't exist without the parents, they're the backbone. They ferry the kids and are there for support for regatta days. York City now is a club very much in the top league. It can hold its own with many of the southern clubs. We are able to make that commitment to training, giving them the right boats and equipment, we get some first class coaches who are mostly volunteers.

But it's a battle. It's not an easy sport. I was talking to a parent the other day and the difference in their son is amazing in just six months. He used to be undisciplined, unwilling to do anything, now he's a totally different person, has a pride in himself, his work has improved, and his attitude to life. I've heard this so many times. Rowing seems to produce something rather special. It opens a door. If you've once rowed, you always want to row. It still draws me down to the river. It's like a magnet. It gets into your blood. When the youngsters have come out of the boat and they've won, they're about whacked. And they're awarded probably the first trophy they've ever had. That means so much. In the 'Small Boats Head' race, the age range was 12 to 82.

1956 Cups Presentation; from left to right: Stuart Gill, Reg Jackson (Captain), Gordon Gill, Ken Woodruff, Ian Gill. (Michael Saville & Brian Snelson)

Stamina is vitally important. You've got to be very strong willed to maintain that determination and not let your colleagues down. I was once sandwiched between a farmer and a marketing man from Rowntree's. If you row between two very powerful people, it keeps you on your toes. It was exhilarating. Great comradeship and not letting your crew down, that's uppermost in your mind. As a nation now we really are excelling in our rowing. We try to encourage all aspects, from those who row competitively, racing most weekends, to the individual who wants to do it as a recreational sport. Rowing has got to find a balance to meet all needs.

HARRY ATKINS

Harry Atkins was born in York in 1927. His brother joined York City Rowing Club in 1935. After national service in the RAF Harry joined the club in 1948 and rowed until 1959. He has been made a life member.

I won an event rowing in a four at York regatta in 1951. I rowed at several regattas away from York, and on three occasions in eights, in the 'Head of the River', over a similar course to the Boat Race. Being a young chap in my 20s, one or two of us were a little bit boisterous [especially] when you get a drop of the amber coloured liquid. The training is much more serious now than in my early days. It's just beyond me, the amount they do now.

We used to look forward to the annual dinner and the regatta dances, usually held at Terry's restaurant. The old boat club was a rickety old building. It didn't lend itself to much on the social side. We had no hot water, and a coke stove in the centre where the lockers were, where we used to change. Used to plonk an old tub on top of the coke stove as a means of heating water. The bar, you opened a cupboard door and sat down on upturned crates. It was rather crude. I remember at a committee meeting many years ago, it was developing into a heated argument as to who should bear the cost of transporting boats and oars to away regattas. There was a chap called Dick Fox who was a gents' outfitter. He quietened things down by saying, "Don't let's get too agitated, gentlemen, after all it's only a game".

Me and the chaps in my crew, we didn't go to the extent of watching diets and rigid training. But some probably did. I would perhaps steer clear of athletes of that denomination! I remember one January, training in this four and we got up by Clifton Scope, and the crew in front of us sank. They were big

York City II - York City rowing club 1950s, Harry Atkins in bow at rear. (Harry Atkins)

lads, they swam to the bank and one of them put the cox on his shoulders and ran back to the boathouse. They were all wet through. I was in the four still afloat and we got the boat in tow and dragged it back. That first eight that I rowed in, in London in 1954, one of the lads couldn't swim. And we had him purposely at number 4 in the centre of the boat, so had we sank on the River Thames, we could watch over him. I was up at the sharp end, at bow. I was one of the light ones. It wasn't much good having a 14 or 15 stoner at the sharp end. We put the heavies in the centre of the boat, and called them the engine room.

There was that terrible period following the fire in 1954 when we'd no base at all. Eventually we did get permission to build a boathouse close to Lendal Bridge. I was joint secretary. When we got moved, we'd no facilities at all. What little bit of rowing that we did, it was thanks to St Peter's School letting us use their boathouse and facilities. By the time we'd got planted in the new boathouse with new equipment, I was nearing the end, I was 29, thinking of hanging my shorts up.

Money was tight. We had a communication from some army officers at Catterick. They wanted to use our facilities. We *decided yes, but we were going to charge them. After all they were going to be using one of our five eights. If one silly devil put his foot through the skin, or if you had a mishap with the blades, it's a costly business getting them repaired. This eight came along, more than once, and I got to know that one of them hadn't paid this fee. I thought, "Right, monkey". I went down to the boathouse. All eight got in the boat and the cox. I said, "Just a moment, excuse me". "Oh yes, yes?", rather la-di-dah they were. "You're the captain? Well I'm the secretary. You haven't paid". "Oh yes, yes, I will do, old boy". So I said, "Yeah, now". "Oh no, not now". I says, "Right, get out of the ... boat", and he did. And that ruined that trip for them!*

When I was training for the London 'Head of the River' which is four and a quarter miles, we'd start training about Christmas time. The climax of our rowing, we'd row up to Poppleton in easy stages. We would turn the boat at the War Memorial then

York City Rowing Club, 1951. L to R: Harry Atkins (bow), Les Newey, Don Sigworth, Ron Simpson (stroke), John Johnston (cox). (Harry Atkins)

*give it some hammer from Poppleton to the Guildhall steps.
But we built up to that. We'd do some training, used to call it
Savage Sunday. We'd row to Nun Monkton which is eight miles,
pull the boat in, leave it on the sandy bank and make our way
to the Alice Hawthorn [pub] for a 'liquid lunch'. I remember
coming back in one piece, eight and a quarter miles. Savage
Sunday! Happy days.*

TOM RANSLEY

York University graduate, Tom Ransley, is York City Rowing club's
rising star. Aged 26, he is aiming for Olympic glory as part of Great
Britain's eight crew in 2012. They won silver at the World Championships at Slovenia to help Great Britain to top the medal table, also
performing well at the World Cup. In the York Press, Tom said that,

*It is reassuring and inspiring to be part of a system and a set-up
that has produced some really outstanding results over the
years. It is something I'm used to through doing the Boat Race
and my time with the GB rowing team. Every year you have to
fight for your seat. It keeps you honest and training as hard as
you can to stay in your seat.*

MAGS FELTER

Mags Felter, who works in the Conservation Laboratory at York
Archaeological Trust, rows with York City Rowing Club.

*The present club is a large, dynamic and friendly one, with
rowers of all ages and abilities. I've been a member for about
six years (having also rowed at York University) and have really
enjoyed training and racing in York and other local regattas
and at national events. In 2009 the women's squad from YCRC
entered an 8+ at Women's Henley regatta, held two weeks before*

York City Rowing Club Women's eight, triumph at Henley. Mags Felter, fourth from left.

(Mags Felter)

York City Rowing Club Women's winning eight at Henley. Mags Felter, third from right.

(Mags Felter)

*Henley Royal Regatta. We had raced shortly before at another
national regatta and knew we were in with a chance of doing
well, but the time trial, to eliminate the slowest crews, was
not our best effort and we were quite nervous. We managed an
excellent start to the race and won* [the time trial]. *The final,
after another win in the third round, was really close but again
our start really worked and we were able to stay ahead and win
by a quarter of a boat length, which seems a very small distance
when the boat is right next to you! It was great to feel that this
win, a first for York City Rowing Club women, could be added
to the many other successes of women's rowing at York.*

JAMIE MACLEOD

Jamie MacLeod was born in 1953 and learnt to row at Bradford
Grammar School. He developed his skill at Cambridge University
where he rowed for their reserve crew, Goldie, which beat the Oxford
reserves, Isis, by five lengths in 1973. He qualified as a GP but decided
to work as a rowing coach.

*In 1974 I won the Prince Philip Cup, the International coxed
four event at Henley Royal Regatta. I represented Great Britain
for the first time in the World Championships in 1974 in the
coxed four in Lucerne and rowed for Cambridge in 1975 beating
Oxford by four lengths. I coached the Cambridge women's
Boat Race crew to beat Oxford and rowed for Great Britain in
the VIII at the World Championships. In 1976 I rowed at the
Montreal Olympics in a pair coming seventh, and rowed for
Great Britain in the coxed pair at the World Championships
in 1977. At the 1980 Olympics I rowed for Great Britain in the
coxed pair, coming ninth.*

*I began to work as a volunteer coach at St. Peter's School in
2003 and was appointed in 2006 as their Director of Rowing.*

Chapter 16

SAILING

Yachting has always been very popular in England, and since sailing was introduced into the Olympic programme in 1900, Great Britain has done remarkably well and won 55 medals, (28 of them gold).

Olympic sailing takes place in the sea, but many clubs in the country sail on rivers. The York Railway Institute Sailing Club, based at Bishopthorpe, started life in the late 1950s. The club house was officially opened in 1964, with a fleet of twelve dinghies. Three new landing stages and a second slipway were added in the early 1970s. In 1983 windsurfers and canoeists were also allowed to join. Members tend to own their own boats but there are several boats available at the club.

MIKE AND ANGELA CRAGGS

Mike Craggs has been a member of the club for over forty years.

A small, friendly, family sailing club, it was formerly known as British Transport Yacht Club, formed in 1957 by British Rail employees. When British Rail was privatised in the 1980s, the club became the York RI Sailing Club. Members can race or just cruise.

Racing is programmed every Sunday from March until October and Wednesday evenings from May until August. The winter series is sailed on a Saturday afternoon from November until Christmas. We have fleet racing (all the same type of dinghies), handicap racing (mixed dinghies), long races, short races, team racing and match racing. And we sail a variety of dinghies including GP14, Lasers, Toppers, Streakers and RS200s.

Mike and Angela Craggs 2006 (Mike and Angela Craggs)

In 1976 Mike Craggs qualified as a Royal Yachting Association Senior Instructor and the club became an RYA Teaching Establishment the following year.

Angela and I joined the Club in March 1970 when we both realised we had an interest in water sports. We learned to sail on the river, following that with a week at a sailing school in Tighnabruaich in Scotland. We bought our GP14, in December 1970. We still sail and race her today. We have run annual sailing courses every year since then. Our son and daughter learned to sail at the Club, starting out in an Optimist then moving on to Toppers. After that they bought their own boats! Both are sailing instructors and help to run the courses with other club members.

We have one member who completed the Round the World Clipper Race. Several members have made sailing their careers. Our daughter Kate (now Skelton) qualified as a professional sailor. She skippered a yacht in the Mediterranean and Caribbean. It was funded by a charity and took under-privileged youngsters on six week trips as part of their Duke of Edinburgh Award. After that she moved on to work as First Mate on various Superyachts.

In June 2011, inspired by the Royal Yacht Association's 'Sail for Gold' programme, York Railway Institute Sailing Club and the Yorkshire Ouse Sailing Club joined forces and organised an event to go right through the centre of York. A fleet of eight boats raced from Skeldergate Bridge to the Millennium Bridge. Although it was June,

Faster - RS200 under spinnaker c2010 (Mike and Angela Craggs)

the weather was a little challenging. Over the four races, Kate Skelton came first in a Topper.

Another member has worked in sailing since leaving university. Recently he has been working in Oman, helping to train some of their Olympic hopefuls, and yet another member went down the professional sailing route working for Neilson's [holiday company] *teaching dinghy and wind surfing. Peter Craggs and Phil Nelson raced at Weymouth, the Olympic sailing venue, in 2011* [in their RS200 dinghy]. *We have two boats going to the GP14 World Championships at Looe in Cornwall in August, 2012. A small claim to fame is that a number of years ago some teenagers from the Club went on a training course in the summer and on the course our son Peter beat the teenage Paul Goodison in a race!* [Paul won gold at the 2008 Olympics].

Racing is an enjoyable way to improve your sailing skills. It has been likened to chess on water as you have to handle the dinghy, read the wind and compete against other boats.

York Railway Institute Sailing Club and flooded Ouse 2012

(Christine Kyriacou)

— *Chapter 17* —
SHOOTING

Olympic shooting has 15 events, featuring shotguns, pistols and rifles. The sport has been contested since 1896, with the exception of 1904 and 1928. There was controversy in 1900 when live pigeons were used in the Olympics in Paris, and over 300 were shot dead.

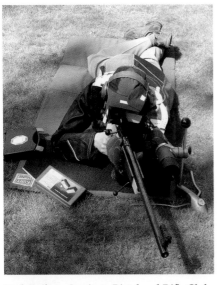

York Railway Institute Pistol and Rifle Club, prone target rifle (Alan Johnson)

Shotgun events consist of skeet, trap and double trap, and competitors move as clay targets are launched into the air. For Pistol and Rifle categories, competitors aim at a 10 ringed target from a set distance (10, 25 or 50 metres), from either kneeling, standing or prone positions.

YORK RAILWAY INSTITUTE PISTOL AND RIFLE CLUB

Tucked away in an old engine shed near York railway station is the York Railway Institute Pistol and Rifle Club, founded in 1908. After the Boer War, where he felt that the English did not shoot well, Frederick, Lord Roberts, decided to set up small bore rifle clubs all over the country to train men in the correct use of guns, which turned out to be very useful in the First World War. The club targets still have a facsimile of the Roberts signature at the top. The York club was affili-

161

ated to the Society of Miniature Rifle Clubs, now the National Small Bore Rifle Association. Other clubs which opened in York in the first decade of the 20th century were the Air Rifle League, and the York Miniature Rifle Club, both in 1907, and the York Gun Club in 1910.

KEITH WOOD

Keith Wood has been a member of the club for 20 years.

We have two ranges, one in the city and an outdoor one at Hessay, a 100 yard one. I used to shoot when I was young, I had two uncles with farms and was introduced at an early age. I was 22 years on York City Council and didn't have the time. But I promised myself when I retired, it would be nice to go back to shooting. I retired in 1992 and started again.

After Hungerford, [the massacre in 1987 when 16 were killed and 15 injured by a gunman with a shocking arsenal of weapons, though all were legal], *pistol shooting was banned and all the pistols taken away. We lost half our members after that. We had an outdoor range and we transferred* [from bullets] *onto black powder. We have 11 booths, targets at 20 yard range. Sport rifles, which are shorter and lighter, became popular.*

Target at York Railway Institute Pistol and Rifle Club 2012 *(Van Wilson)*

George Taylor, York Railway Institute Pistol and Rifle Club (Van Wilson)

There is very strict governance of firearms and a limit on the amount of ammunition. The UK Olympic team has to train in Switzerland. There is a special arrangement for guns coming in. In our club we have application forms, there have to be references, and people need to testify to your state of mind. There is a six month probationary period, you learn safe practices, shoot under close supervision and a log is kept with comments. You need good attendance over six months then you can apply to be a member. We advise the police who are the licensing authorities, you then apply for a firearms licence and buy a rifle.

The police will check your home for safe storage. We have 94 members, with a growing handful of women.

We have competitions at county and national level. Members have won gold, silver and bronze. We shoot at the same distance as the Olympics, prone, standing or bench rest position. For the prone rifle, you are laid down, like a traditional marksman. We have teams in the Yorkshire league and the Cumbrian league. You can buy a second hand rifle for £150. You can get super rifles for £2000! Ammunition, for competition shooting, you would use a max of 50 rounds. The competition is done through the post, all targets (cards) are sent in to an independent person. Or there can be competitions on a set day at a club, but you can do it without travelling. In a competition you wouldn't shoot more than three cards, your accuracy gets less.

We have shooting every night, with different disciplines, Monday lightweight sports rifle, Tuesday prone shooting on

York Railway Institute Pistol and Rifle Club black powder pistols (Alan Johnson)

mats [of small bore rifles], *Wednesday is a mix, Thursday air rifles, Friday air pistols. Hessay is available seven days a week.*

One of the most successful members of the club was E B (Dick) Fogg, secretary for 40 years. On the wall of the office is a collection of badges and medals awarded to him, including Remington 400 Palma and the elite British 400 club, which he means that he scored 4 x 100s on the Dewar course, the maximum score possible. (The course consists of 20 shots at 50 metres and 20 at 100 yards). He died in June 1987.

Early in 2012 the club reopened after refurbishment. New shooting booths have been installed and the area behind the targets (Linotex which is like a rubber curtain), through which the shots pass, has been modernised to meet the specifications of the National Rifle Association.

The Railway Institute gave financial support and we put our own money in. We have modern standards, the latest safety

York Railway Institute Pistol and Rifle Club. Dick Fogg, far left, middle row. 1954

features and improved lighting. It used to be in semi-dilapidated conditions. The Lord Mayor came to fire the first shot at the unveiling in January.

Rifle shooting has four divisions for team events. There are 22 divisions for the air pistol. Division I members average 185-190 out of a score of 200, whereas lower divisions will average 120. But medals can be won in any divisions and members of the club are encouraged to fire competitively.

Three members of the club are in the Yorkshire county team, using prone rifles. Two are in the air pistol category. One member won the bench rest category at Bisley, 'Europe's premier shooting venue' in Sussex, the first year it started. The national association is working hard to allow disabled shooters to participate more, including bringing in shooting for the blind which now takes place in 20 centres, using a technical system which can marry up light to a sound system. The shooter can use an assistant to help with targeting.

Ammunition for Ruger Rifle and shotgun

(Martin Pinder)

— *Chapter 18* —
SWIMMING

Men's swimming has been contested in the Olympic Games since 1896. Britain has won 34 medals. Women's swimming started in 1912. Only eight British women have won gold medals. York-born Anita Lonsbrough won in 1960 and it took 48 years for the next, Rebecca Adlington, who won two gold medals in Beijing in 2008.

Of all Olympic sports, swimming is the one most associated with York, which has produced a number of excellent swimmers, including Olympians. The earliest public swimming baths mentioned in the city are those owned by the Yorkshire Philosophical Society at the Marygate end of the Museum Gardens, which opened in 1837, and

Old Yearsley swimming pool c 1910 (City of York Council, Local Studies Collection)

closed in the early 1920s. Prior to that there was, of course, swimming in the river and the Yorkshire Gazette reported in 1828 that women were 'offended by men bathing in the Ouse'.

YEARSLEY BATHS

The York Yearsley Amateur Swimming Club was based on a stretch of the River Foss on Huntington Road from 1860, with the bed of the river paved for a hundred yards. A shed was erected, and an attendant engaged to look after the club. The 'pool' (known as Old Yearsley Baths) was open to males only. Edmund Wilson (who left a bequest towards swimming facilities in York) swam there as a boy, as did Reg Butler. (Reg also played in the Rowntree's baseball team just after the Second World War, the only team known of in the city). Reg recalls,

You dived in off the bank, a swallow dive, you didn't do a deep dive or you'd hit the bottom. I was a good swimmer, good runner, [with York Harriers], good at all sports but champion

Rowntree's baseball team 1947, Reg Butler first left on back row, next to brother Eric
(*Reg Butler*)

Reg Butler in training for York Harriers (Reg Butler)

at nothing. Both ends of the Foss were sieved so that no dogs and cats could come through, and occasionally they scraped the bottom and mud out of it. They had a few members but anybody could swim there, skinny dipping, not many had a costume. There was an open hut with seats round and you got changed in there, you paid half a crown to become a member, a lot of money then. But you always got pick pockets. If you had any money, it wasn't there when you came back. I was a boy in 1921, I got a medal for beating men. There was a lad that could always beat me, he lived in Hungate, and a lot of those lads swam there, the water from the Electric Works running into the Foss was always warm, and they were never out of it, real water babies.

The new Yearsley Baths was built near to Rowntree's factory and presented to the city in 1909. In 1959 the charges were 9d, and 4d for children. Rowntree employees used the pool between 12 and 2pm. Rowntree Park open-air baths opened in 1924 and closed in 1980. A public campaign did not prevent the baths from demolition. Now the only public pools are Yearsley's, though its future is uncertain, Energise in Cornlands Road and Waterworld at Monks Cross.

WILFRED WOODCOCK

There were also swimming competitions in the River Ouse. The York-shire Gazette of July 1933 reported that,

Wilfred Woodcock of York City Swimming Club [the uncle of Dennis Wood-cock, featured in Chapter 23, Water Polo] *will defend his title tomorrow at the Yorkshire river swim in the Ouse. Four York swimmers and 11 others are entered for the race from Clifton Scope to Blue Bridge.*

A week later,

Woodcock retained the Yorkshire Amateur Swimming Association mile and three quarter championship in the Ouse for the second year running, in 42 minutes. There was a thrilling struggle between Woodcock and Cyril Jackson. Both used the double over arm stroke. In the last few hundred yards, the extra stamina of Woodcock won the day.

YORK CITY BATHS CLUB AND ST GEORGE'S SWIMMING BATHS

The City Corporation applied to the 'Local Government Board' in 1878 for £3000 to erect public baths. Water would be taken from the upper level of the Foss where 'water was good' and pumping appa-ratus had been arranged in case of drought. The plans were approved and St George's swimming baths in St George's Field opened in 1880. York Amateur Swimming and Humane Society was founded in 1882. This amalgamated with York Baths Club to become York City Baths Club. In the 1950s costumes could be hired for 3d, soap cost 2d and Brylcreem was 2d a shot. St George's is particularly remembered for the abundance of chlorine, and a large number of York school children of the time learnt to swim there. There were various problems though. After a flood, (a regular occurrence because the baths were close to the river), the pools took two weeks to clean out and rats had to be caught

St George's Baths 1911 (City of York Council, Local Studies Collection)

before it re-opened. Then in 1960, leaks in the baths held up training for York Olympic candidates. St George's was demolished in 1972.

In 1959 the Council passed plans for a new state of the art swimming pool near Skeldergate Bridge, to be 14 feet above ground because of flooding. The main pool would be 110 x 48 feet, with a range of diving boards, and a learner's pool to be 30 x 12 feet, with seating for 1000 spectators, offices, coffee lounge and club room, with air conditioning and purifiers. Unfortunately the pool never came into being, because there was an objection by the government. In 1961 plans were passed for the Edmund Wilson pool in Thanet Road, built on land bequeathed as a 'recreational facility'. Yet that pool was demolished in 2009 and a supermarket built.

York City Baths Club still continues today teaching children to swim from as young as four.

LONZ WEBSTER AND YORK SWIMMERS

Alonzo Crystal Webster (known as Lonz) had been a middleweight boxer before he came to York in the 1920s, with many fights all over England and as far afield as Denmark. He became superintendent and coach at York City Baths Club in 1929. During his time there, the Club produced some very high calibre swimmers.

In August 1957, three York swimmers, Peter Kendrew, Terry Boyes and Elspeth Ferguson, were selected for the Great Britain team. Peter, aged 16, was chosen to swim in the 100 yards freestyle against Sweden. He had won the boys 110 yard freestyle and 110 yards backstroke final at the age of 15, and was the fastest swimmer to qualify for the final of boys 220 yards freestyle championship. He went on to

Roddy Frame, Alan Clarkson, Terry Boyes, Pete Kendrew 1958 (Pauline Clarkson)

St George's Baths 1952. Pauline Musgrove is second from right. (Pauline Clarkson née Musgrove)

*1948 Fishergate Primary Girls' Swimming Team. L to R – Back, Miss D Lord, Violet Mal-
linson, Anne Smith, Jean French, Joyce Rhodes, unknown, Beryl Benson, unknown, Dorothy
Bond, Mr H Rayson, headmaster. Front – unknown, Barbara Stannard, Doreen Pheasey,
Maureen Chevens, Valerie Jackson, Jean Rhodes.* (Maureen Chevens)

swim in the 1960 Rome Olympics and at the 1962 Commonwealth Games won two bronze and one silver medal. He was the oldest participant in the Great Britain team at the Tokyo Olympic Games in 1964, at the tender age of 24! In the 1970s he became the manager of St John's College pool.

Elspeth Ferguson went to the Commonwealth Games and was European games silver medallist in the 100 yards freestyle relay team. In the 1958 European Championships, she

Pauline Clarkson, Pete Kendrew, Pam Lester in 1992, Olympians honoured by the International Olympic Committee (Pauline Clarkson)

was part of the four women freestyle relay team. Her routine was to swim a mile at 7am, a mile at midday and a mile in the evening, and in the season she swam eight miles a day.

Another York swimmer who went to the Olympics was Pamela Johnson, later Lester, who swam in the 400 metres individual medley aged 16, in Tokyo in 1964.

TERRY BOYES

I swam for six years frontline. One of our big trips, Elspeth and I went to compete in China. Chou en-Lai, [Chinese Premier 1949–1976], came to the pool to see the international championship and I asked the interpreter if I could borrow a flash to take a photo. Chou en-Lai beckoned me over. He spoke in pigeon English, and said, "Are you going to the October 1st big parade?", a big military parade there. I said yes, it was a double

York Swimming Team at national championships 1955. Back row: Alan Clarkson, unknown, Elspeth Ferguson, Jim Wright at end. Middle: Kath Maloney, Margaret Wright, unknown. Front: Pauline Musgrove, Brooke Midgeley, Wendy Andrews (Brooke Midgeley)

celebration as it was my birthday. It got to the day and I got a wickerwork basket full of carnations and two birthday cakes, one iced in English and one iced in Chinese.

The Germans started master swimming in five year blocks. When you were 25, you moved into the next block. I pioneered the route to Germany and the USA and Canada for these championships. I had one or two sponsors and could go to the championships there. I swam in the Masters, but the Amateur Swimming Association said I had been swimming against professionals in the US, so wouldn't let me swim at the British national championships. I took a banner protesting about it, it was ridiculous. I wrote to the Prime Minister and the Queen, I had a letter back from her equerry saying although they sympathised, they couldn't do much about it.

Terry was manager of Frances Scaife Swimming Pool in Pocklington in 1970 and manager of the Edmund Wilson pool in 1978. By then he had competed in the Empire and Commonwealth Games and many international competitions. He won gold medals at the Masters championships in Tokyo and Brisbane.

I used to do 100 metre freestyle, 200 and 400 metre freestyle, 400 individual medley and 100 metre butterfly. I held the Master's championships at the Edmund Wilson pool and people came from Germany, America and all over.

Lonz Webster was forced by illness to retire prematurely in early 1959. The council gave him a presentation, describing him as 'the finest coach in Yorkshire and one of the finest in the country'. The Yorkshire Evening Press reported that, 'He has made York City Baths Club the most powerful in the country. The greatest single factor of the outstanding success is the tenacity, almost fanaticism, of the superintendent'. In ten years Lonz helped to win 120 Yorkshire championships and eight nationals. He died, aged 63, only a few months after retirement.

Maureen Chevens explains that,

The value of his work is incalculable and should be greatly acclaimed. He was teacher and coach to York schoolchildren, many of whom became county and national champions. More than a few became international and some even Olympic competitors.

Probably the best tribute to Lonz was that the Club continued to produce excellent swimmers. In 1961 it was said to 'enhance York's reputation the world over'. George Lester was coaching the elementary classes, and Derek Stubbs the intermediate and advanced classes. Amazingly at this time the club had 750 members, 400 under 12. When asked for the secret of its success, the reply was that 'we have eight or nine officials who do tremendous voluntary work with great enthusiasm with the objective of development and advancement of swimming'. The club began to campaign for a better swimming pool, with more adequate facilities. The York and District Schools' Athletic Association now awards a Lonz Webster trophy for swimming.

DEREK STUBBS

Derek Stubbs was a leading figure in swimming in Britain for over 30 years before his death in 2011. He learnt to swim at eight at St George's, and became a coach and later chief coach at the York City Baths Club. He was the Amateur Swimming Association's first Director of Swimming as well as representing Yorkshire at water polo from 1947 to 1963. Derek was chief coach for the England team at the Commonwealth Games in 1970. On his 80th birthday in 2008, he raised over £1300 for the Yorkshire Air Ambulance by swimming 80 lengths.

PAULINE MUSGROVE AND ALAN CLARKSON

Pauline Musgrove was born in 1936 and competed in the 110 metres backstroke at the Helsinki Olympics in 1952. But she started swimming at the age of nine. Her daughter Karen Burdass tells her story.

In those days the river played a big part in York. Swimming was a life skill that people needed. Once she was in the pool, it was clear that she was going to be quite adept at swimming.

The Baths Club was a huge thing in York. Lonz Webster was a big part of it, his coaching wasn't paid for, it came from his love of swimming. He lived in the flat above. On a weekend he would take the younger ones, to teach them to swim. The Club swimmers, as a sort of repayment, helped him. There were two pools, one round and one rectangular.

177

St George's baths 1952. Pauline Musgrove tells children about going to the Olympic Games
(Pauline Clarkson)

Mum was 15 when she qualified for the 1952 Olympics. They had the nationals all round the country but you had to qualify. Now they have age groups, then they only had junior, 16 and below, and senior. It was usually unheard of that a junior would qualify. She qualified in the nationals and won the juniors at Hove. So they put her in for the Olympic trials, Blackpool June '52. Nowadays you start doing trials a year before. She trained every night. When they did a freestyle event, you can do any stroke. Most people do front crawl because it's the quickest, but Mum would do backstroke because it was quicker than anybody else's front crawl. She could do a freestyle event in Leeds and then go to a backstroke event in Sheffield on the same day. Mum was the first one, with Lonz Webster,

York's Lord Mayor (Alderman Harwood) presents trophy to some of Yorkshire Schools Division 3 junior girls swimming team after first All-England Schools Championship. L to R: Maureen Chevens (York), Shirley Marles (Leeds), Pauline Musgrove (York), Pam Cockcroft (Hull) (Maureen Chevens)

to do the backstroke flip turn. Come in, legs flick over, and go out on your back. Touch and turn. That was quite a big thing. Everybody was going, "Ooh. What was that?" Lonz was a very cheerful man, and very encouraging. Not everybody liked him, he could be quite forceful. If you're driven as a sports person, you need that. Maybe that's what gives you the edge. Lonz was ahead of his time in some of his coaching. My mother was extremely positive about him. From his point of view, she was maybe the star swimmer of her age group.

The family could not afford to go to the Olympics with Pauline.

But the Press did a whip round, and the whole of York donated money for them to go. They raised so much that Lonz Webster was able to go as well. It was incredible. Purely through the generosity of people in York. And the letters that people wrote, what regard they held her in.

The nationals and the Olympic trials all happened within months of each other. At the Olympics she didn't swim very well and she was disappointed. She was expected to do great things, I think it was just the pressure.

Mum didn't compete again after Helsinki. She went to work at Rowntree's and she stopped swimming in 1959. She met my father, [Alan Clarkson], at the Club in 1953. They got married in 1959. Dad's career was just starting as Mum's was finishing.

Pauline Musgrove goes to Helsinki Olympics 1952, seen off by parents and Lonz Webster second from right. (Pauline Clarkson)

Pauline Musgrove with trophies, 1952 (Pauline Clarkson)

But in 1960 Mum was asked to be chaperone for the GB team. In '72 she was chaperone for the Olympics.

Alan Clarkson was born in 1936 and attended Nunthorpe Grammar School in York. He represented England in the

Commonwealth Games at Cardiff, with Pete Kendrew, Terry Boyes, Roddie Frame, and Don Andrews. Dad did national service and they stationed him at Linton on Ouse. He used to swim before work, get the eight o'clock bus, back on the five o'clock and then swim again.

Alan was Yorkshire 200 metres and 400 metres freestyle champion in 1959 and 1,500 metres champion for five years. When his competitive days ended, he became coach from 1959 to 1968. Then,

Pauline and Alan Clarkson, 1959
(Pauline Clarkson)

Wedding of Alan Clarkson and
Pauline Musgrove, 1959, with
Don Andrews, Pete Kendrew,
Terry Boyes (Pauline Clarkson)

Dad became team manager, he took the team in 1970 to the Commonwealth Games. In 1972 Dad was asked to build FINA, the world swimming organisation. He was team manager in 1976 to the Montreal Olympics, [as well as internationals and the Commonwealth Games in 1970, 1974 and 1978, and world championships in 1973, 1975 and 1978. He was also a race judge at the Olympics in 1980, 1984, 1988 and 1992]. *Many weeks a year would have been taken out doing all that and that's aside from the administration. He used to bring a training camp to St John's pool. He went to every Olympics until 2008. If you're passionate about something you just do it. It was in his blood. Nothing would have pleased him more than being at Beijing and seeing Rebecca Adlington win, or in 1976 seeing David Wilkie win. Actually seeing the rewards, the swimmers doing well. He wasn't paid, they had expenses paid and he would pay for my mum to go. She knew a lot of people in the swimming world so they shared the experience.*

Alan Clarkson became the first person in history to receive a long service award from the British Olympic Association, presented by Princess Anne, after being on the committee for 21 years.

He got the OBE in 2004. He stepped down in 2007, he thought it would be better for younger blood to come through. And he had an accountancy business to run, it was unfair on his clients. I know school swimming is not as prevalent, which I think is terrible. I was nine when I started to swim, started to compete at ten, the Barbican was our pool. My brother swam although he was more a water polo player and runs water polo

Alan Clarkson 1958, (in Empire and Commonwealth Games blazer) with trophies.

(Pauline Clarkson)

in York. Mum coached and Dad coached, it was just our world. Being brought up with it, I used to travel around with them to training camps or meets. It was exciting. Swimming on a recreational level, if it's not the top sport, it's certainly the second. And it's just not encouraged in York. Yearsley's a fantastic pool, they have spent money on it and it's much better, but they were talking of closing that down as well.

Mum and I used to have a swim school, we taught at St Peter's one night and one night at St John's. When we found out St John's was being knocked down for the new development, there was nowhere else in York to get any pool space. Now I'm a

Brooke Midgeley and Pauline Musgrove on BSA 250 motorbike. (Brooke Midgeley)

swimming coach for St Peter's, the girls. We've had a new pool built there, and Baths Club hire that a lot of nights. We used to go to Edmund Wilson, it was a fantastic pool, and it's been knocked down. The hoops that we had to go through to get planning to build St Peter's pool then they let them just knock down Edmund Wilson!

BROOKE MIDGELEY

Brooke Midgeley was born in York in 1935.

I learnt to swim about the age of five in St George's Baths. It's where I did all the training, with the 'dedicated lunatics'. In summer we swam in the river and anywhere we could find. I must have been about 11 when I got involved with the Club. Fishergate Secondary School had a swimming team. We won the school championships.

Brooke started competing at the age of 12,

In city and county championships. Individuals would compete in games and accrue points. There was one period when we were training for an hour before work, half an hour at lunchtime. Then Lonz opened the pool at nine and we trained for a couple of hours after night school. That was four or five nights a week and Sunday mornings.

At St George's it was a 25 yard pool, so you'd four lengths for 100 yards. There was only one place I remember swimming that was worse and that was a mill pool in Hebden Bridge. It was in the boiler house and it was a trench full of really hot water. You couldn't see anything because it was cloudy. Terry [Boyes] swam smack into the end of it and knocked himself out. That was one of the rounds of Yorkshire championships.

Once [at St George's] *we were swimming butterfly and Jim was coming down the lane by the side of me in the opposite direction. And his arm came over the rope and smacked me across the face. He knocked me out and when I came round, I was lying in a pool of blood and Lonz had chucked me into the shower and turned the cold on and left me there. About 40 years later, I'd been having migraines and the doctor thought it was to do with that. So they filleted my nose.*

At one point we had over 50 per cent of the UK team. It was never the same after Lonz died. He used the same philosophy as he would have done for boxers – work, work, work, work, work.

You had specialisms. Pauline was a backstroker, Alan and Terry swam crawl. He could turn in a very quick 100 metres. For a long time I had the 440 yard record for individual medley because I could swim good crawl, butterfly, pretty good breaststroke and passable backstroke. And the great thing was they only held it once, after that they shortened the length.

Brooke thinks that there is something special about athletes who get as far as the Olympic Games.

There's something that these people have, who are consistently able to turn something out that nobody else can. Given the same piece of kit, they can still get more out of it than anyone else.

Now all the athletes are professional. The Amateur Swimming Association were really keen. One year at the nationals, it was Speedo I think, they'd given us all swimming trunks and the girls costumes and we had to give them back because the ASA reckoned that you were infringing your amateur status, and you were advertising. Even the amount of flesh you were allowed to show from your costumes, that was regulated.

MAUREEN CHEVENS

Maureen Chevens began swimming at school. In 1946 she was awarded a bronze medallion engraved with the city coat of arms, for swimming her 'length'. At Fishergate Primary School she won the York Girls Junior Schools trophy, and was junior champion in 1948. She went on to win various awards.

Mr James of Fishergate senior school was team manager of York schools swimming teams. When we had to travel anywhere, everything was arranged for us, so neatly and well that it

1948 York Schools Swimming Champions at St George's. L to R: John Crane (14), Scarcroft (Secondary boys champion); James Wright (11), Glen Primary (Junior boys champion); Rita Matson (13), Mill Mount Grammar (Secondary girls champion); Maureen Chevens (11) (junior girls champion). (Maureen Chevens)

was never questioned. Our mentors well deserved the thanks they got. In my five years in the Division Three schools team competing in the 'National Schools', we swam in London, Blackpool, Bournemouth, Bristol and Lancaster. I was entered, while at Fishergate, in the Proficiency Test. This involved swimming and diving skills and a life-saving carry as well as a length of each stroke, back stroke and front crawl, plain dive, racing dive, plunge and a trick in the water. There was a trophy for the pupil with the highest marks. The badge wasn't easily come by and we wore it with pride.

1953 St George's, Yorkshire Schools Swimming Championships. Back row: Victor Smeeton, Maxine Hendry, Colin Calpin, John Kendrew, Janet Livesey, Ian Rawson, Ann Rhodes, Michael Simpson, Brian Precious*, Janet Denton, Brian Bulmer. Middle: M James (Fishergate Senior School), unknown, Anne Surgenor, Pat Holland, Valerie Carruthers, Wendy Andrews*, Kath Maloney, unknown, unknown, Janet Bell, Margaret Wright, Lonz Webster. Front: Alan Clarkson, Eileen Barrett, Malcolm Sandilands*, Maureen Chevens*, Anne Golledge, Carole White, Barbara Trim, Peter Kendrew. (Pauline Musgrove, Colin Burley, Donald Andrews and Roddy Frame missing from picture.) * individual winners
(Maureen Chevens)

188

1950 was a particularly successful year. 14 girls and 14 boys from York schools swam in Hull. The York team won seven individual championships and six team championships. I did swim for the county as well as Yorkshire Schools.

A team from Yorkshire schools competed against Midland counties, and 12 York swimmers were in the team. We won the match by 133 points to 58. Pauline Musgrove won one of the individual firsts. In 1951 there was an Olympic training scheme weekend in which five York swimmers were invited to take part, Eddie Clemit, John White, Rita Matson, Pauline Musgrove and myself.

Maureen was county schools 100 yards champion for five consecutive years.

At the fourth English Schools Swimming Association championships at Bournemouth, my very kind hostess was Mrs Tanner, a partly sighted lady who had a delightful little grandson. His name was Jimmy, she called him Sixpence, a play on the surname. We were so lucky meeting such lovely people wherever our competitions took us.

In 1966, Maureen was asked to be one of the team managers for the Division Three Team in Cardiff.

They were grand days. Those of us who swam for York and Yorkshire Schools, Division Three, did so with enormous pride and when we won, we did so with great delight and a fierce joy.

Her association with sport ran from 1946 to the 1970s. As a teacher at Mill Mount, (until 1974) she was involved with the York Schools Athletic Association swimming section (see also Athletics Chapter) to which her contribution was enormous.

Bronze length medallion; Winner's award from English Schools swimming championships;
York Schools Athletic Association badge for proficiency in swimming (Maureen Chevens)

"LIMPET"
The Original
STRAPLESS SWIM CAP
WITH STENCILLED BADGE

For better swimming!

NORTH'S RUBBER CO. LTD.
131 WESTERN ROAD · MITCHAM

Swimming cap advert, 1960

In 1967 the chairman Mr F W Lund, appealed for St George's baths to be replaced by one of Olympic standard, adding that the outstanding record of the city's swimmers proved that they deserved it. In the '60s and '70s members Amanda Radnage, Ann Barner, Elizabeth Shaw, Roderick Frame, Cathy Dunn all swam for England.

Ann Barner won two silver medals in the 1966 Commonwealth Games. Amanda Radnage was part of the Great Britain team against Holland at Blackpool in

1967, and selected for training for the Mexico Olympics in 1968. She did not take part in 1968 but went on to win a bronze medal in the Edinburgh Commonwealth Games in 1970. She was then selected for the women's 200 metres at the Munich Olympic Games in 1972. Amanda retired in 1973.

Alan Clarkson and English team, Amanda Radnage on right (Pauline Clarkson)

CAROLINE FOOT

Another Baths Club member, Caroline Foot, won the bronze medal at the 1997 European Championships 100 metres medley relay. She represented Great Britain at the Olympics in 1988 and 1996 (when she was 31) in the 100 metres butterfly and the 100 metres medley relay.

DENNIS WOODCOCK

Dennis Woodcock, who was born in 1933, features in the chapters on diving and water polo, but was also a keen York swimmer. In the last 18 years he has been teaching disabled people to swim and to snorkel, and,

eventually we did four trips out to Elat in Israel to swim with the dolphins. They all enjoyed that. It was fantastic.

He was invited to a Buckingham Palace garden party.

We were stood behind the rope. The chap in front, dressed in morning coat, asked us, "Why are you here?" "I think it's because of swimming with disabled people and dolphins in

191

Israel". "I think the Queen would like to know about that". The Queen came down doing a zigzag talking to people who'd been picked out by her equerries. She shook hands and talked to us for about five minutes. I told her about, "A chap called Colin. He was left for dead on the road, a hit and run driver. His legs were not usable. When we got in the sea, and I was looking after six of them, I saw he had water in his mask and he was moving towards the pontoon so he could put his elbow on it and clear his mask. As I swam to help him, a dolphin went and put its nose between his legs and lifted him up. And just stayed there flipping its tail and keeping him up". She said, "My word, they do have an affinity with humans don't they? That would be in the Red Sea where it's real salty wouldn't it?" I said, "No, ma'am, I think that's the Dead Sea". And she said, "Oh yes, how silly of me". There were about 6,000 at the garden party, and just by chance that happened. It was lovely.

Dennis was awarded a 'Services to Sport' award in 2004, and was referred to as 'York's Mr Sport'.

SYNCHRONISED SWIMMING

This is the only exclusively female Olympic sport. Known as 'water ballet', it was contested for the first time in 1948, and was popularised through Hollywood movie star Esther Williams in the 1940s and '50s. Britain has won no medals for the sport, which has been dominated by Russia. There was some synchronised swimming in York in 1984 but it did not prove very popular.

Chapter 19

TABLE TENNIS

Table tennis started as an after-dinner game played by the aristocracy. It became very popular with young people between the wars, and in 1931 was proposed as an Olympic sport, but there was too much opposition. Agreement was not reached until 1988.

The first mention in York, is of the York Ping Pong Club in the Yorkshire Gazette of April 1902, 'Good after-dance of members and friends for match with Scarborough Bachelors in the Assembly Rooms, decorated with club colours of scarlet and white. Victory for York by 338 points. Bartley's band played an excellent programme of music'.

CATHY MITTON
York table tennis player Cathy Mitton was one of the first athletes to be named for the Great Britain table tennis team for the 2008 Paralympic Games.

Cathy Mitton (Cathy Mitton)

Cathy contracted polio at the age of two. So sport has not been easy for her. But she has persevered and battled against adversity.

There were epidemics of polio in the 1940s and '50s, and lots of people were affected. I had polio when I was a child and the Polio Games had an event every year. You took part in everything, javelin, discus, running and swimming. Now if you're in the elite sports, you're actively discouraged from doing other sports.

Of all the sports I'd tried, table tennis was the only thing I was really any good at. I used to play standing up but I had to start playing in a wheelchair because I couldn't keep my balance. I started playing more frequently in the late 1980s. They'd have a Yorkshire event and winners would go to the national games in Stoke Mandeville. It wasn't until the Paralympics in the 1960s that different disability groups had somewhere further to go.

But initially Cathy had to play against able bodied people.

I found it difficult to find places. Being in a wheelchair, people didn't want to play you. It wasn't inclusive. You could play as long as you brought your own partner. At one point there were national competitions and I was the only representative for the whole of Yorkshire and Humberside. I used to go to Pindarfields Hospital and we put a team in the local league, it was the only way to get any different opponents.

There are so many things to overcome that people don't think about, unless it applies to them. Cathy would get to a place to practise, and find the hall was up lots of steps or at the top of a hill, or the gate would be padlocked, or the lift would not work. It was also difficult to find coaches who could train wheelchair users.

You have to be really really determined if you want to get into it. In 1994 there was an international championship at Stoke Mandeville, that was my first time against international opposition. Then I was selected for the European championships in 1997 in Sweden [where she won silver].

Cathy Mitton (York Press)

Cathy has won three World Championship medals, including gold in Taipei in 2002, and bronze medals at the Sydney and Athens Paralympics Games. In the Beijing Paralympics in 2008, the highlight was appearing in a country whose national game is table tennis.

There were crowds at very session, every seat was taken. There's always going to be people who say it's not real sport [the Paralympics] *and it shouldn't be given any publicity.*

I think the whole point of the Paralympics is for the more disabled people because that is the only thing they've got. When you select somebody who could compete in the able bodied games, you're denying somebody who could never do that.

Cathy played in her third Paralympics at the age of 51, and her determination and desire to show what can be done have proved her to be a true role-model for sportsmen and women with disabilities who want to compete at the highest level.

DAVID POOLE

David Poole started to play the game,

In 1952 as a young lad of 12 and carried on for 21 years. I joined the York Boys' Club in Redeness Street in about 1950. Table tennis was one of the main recreations. The club had been active from pre-war days. The York Table Tennis League had been formed in 1927, one of the earliest structured leagues in the country. There were four adult leagues, junior and ladies' leagues. The junior league consisted of one or two youth clubs

York Table Tennis team 1966.
L to R: Bill Hulmes, Denis Norburn, Frank Gregoire, David Poole. *(David Poole)*

and people like the Railway Institute juniors. By the mid 1950s it was decided to do away with the women's league and juniors. They found their own level of class and ability within five or six senior leagues.

I played for the Boys' Club for about four years. As I got better, I played for the York Railway Institute. I started work in 1956 for the City Council in the offices. NALGO, the National Association of Local Government Officers, ran two or three teams in the league. I played for them for ten seasons. We played for a couple of years in the old workhouse dining hall, it belonged to the council. Every time we had a match we had to clear tables to one side but then we played in a room in the Seahorse in Fawcett Street, then the civil defence store in Nunnery Lane. It had been an old chapel, then a store for camp beds and field cooking stoves and emergency equipment for a wartime evacuation.

David went on to play for the York men's team for some years,

competing with teams from Wakefield and Scarborough and second teams of larger cities, like Huddersfield, Halifax and Dewsbury. There was usually a team of three. You played everybody so you had nine single matches and finished off with a doubles.

In the Yorkshire men's team were

Billy Hulmes, for many years he ran the fish and chip shop at Copmanthorpe, Denis Norburn, an ex-Halifax man and Francis (Frank) Gregoire, a Barbadian, who came to York about 1958 to do a nursing course. When he first came, it was probably a cold night in November, he had two pairs of long trousers on, he took one pair off to play in and put them back on to go out into the cold night air.

*In the Yorkshire league it was four people. It was a different
structure, maybe seven matches a year. You had a bit of travelling. It was mainly a winter sport. They did produce a summer
league but it could get quite hot in summer playing indoors.
A lot of clubs* [in York] *had teams. A good club like Tang Hall,
based at Tang Hall Hotel, their A and B teams were in the
same league. The team for RAF Acaster Malbis were generally
conscription men. The RAF had table tennis players from all
over the country. The North Eastern Electricity had a team, the
Sugar Beet, (a fella called Colin Cook played for them, he's now
a theatre director with the Royal Shakespeare Company. He
was in my class at school), County Hospital, Rowntree's and
Clifton youth clubs, the Deaf Institute, and Southlands Methodist Chapel. St John's College had teams of good standing,
drawn from all over England.*

In 1956-57 David was junior singles champion and junior doubles
with Eric Mortimer. Then,

*I won the men's singles in 1958 and I won the juniors in the
same year* [one of the few men to win both]. *In the county
juniors we were playing against the other northern counties.
We were a bit limited. You only met up with them on the day
because they were living quite a way away.*

*The annual sub was ten shillings, 50p. The tables cost £39, a
month's wages for a tradesman. They were sturdy and they
folded down. Bats were about ten shillings.*

*The equipment's changed a lot. In our day it was 95 per cent
playing with pimpled rubber on wood. A few people played with
a thin coating of sponge. In about 1959, '60, the sandwich bats
came in, a layer of sponge with a layer of rubber. That made a
hell of a difference. I kept to the pimpled rubber. But it was a*

revolution in the sport. The way it's played now, you need a lot of room. In some places we played in, you were restricted. At the Co-op on the Mount we played in a little timber asbestos garage.

Before the war there was an old fella, the secretary of Tang Hall Club. For a year or two they played in his council house bedroom in Melrosegate. They eventually went to play in the original Tang Hall Hotel. In our day we'd have expeditions out to Linton once a season, we'd get the Pullman service bus from Exhibition Square. Not many of them had cars.

CLIVE WARLEY

Clive Warley was born near Malton and came to York in 1958.

I first played table tennis in Wales in the war. As kids you had nothing to do. We got a piece of wood and a ball and just hit it across the table. As soon as I came to York, I joined the Methodist League. I played for Grove's Methodist for two years then in the York and District League for New Earswick Youth Club. From there to Groves Working Men's Club, West Yorkshire Road Car Company then Fulford Road Working Men's Club. To start off there was about 18 clubs, we're down to a few now.
I was a competitive player throughout my career. That was all in my attitude, 'keep going until the fat lady sings', I think is the term.

I've more or less finished playing because of my disability. I found I couldn't move around as much. [He has paralysed legs and wears callipers]. *I stood up. I did have one spell of sitting down. When you've played stood up, you go for things without thinking. Of course I went over and the chair went with me. A lot of people would play wide for a time. But because I stood up*

Clive Warley, chosen as an Olympic torch bearer in 2012 (Clive Warley)

to the table, the angles were cut off, so they had to be excellent players who could do that. Over a period of time you combat that, you find ways of answering their play.

You have profiles when you're a disabled person in sport. I was profile 17, in class 6. But if they found you were too good for that, they could move you up. If you played people with better mobility, it soon showed. The British Sport for the Disabled have an Ethics Committee who get in touch with the hospital, the physiotherapists at the hospital judge you. If you ever won anything, they pull you back and re-test you to make sure. If you're on medication which I never was, you have to declare what you're on. Disabled sport is more rigorously tested than anybody else and if they do find anything, other than what they expect with the medication you're on, you're out. I'm a great believer in the doping system. If there are cheats they should be taken out of the game.

Going back many years, I was asked to attend a tournament for a selection for national championship. We were classified then as the north east. I went up and won it. It came to the doubles, no trouble again, won it. The year after, I was asked to go to Hull to the trials and I came out top and for the next ten years I played for Yorkshire and Humberside. We won the trophy nine times out of ten.

In the [national] *disabled championships I got to the semi-final twice, eight times to the final, and I won five of them. I couldn't go to all the national tournaments. I had a mortgage to pay so the money wasn't available. It meant going away weekends. I was always a floating player because I didn't have ranking points. So at the end of a tournament, I would go from nowhere up to number two or three, and the most I went to was number one. But I wasn't a fulltime player. Early on people thought they could take it easy and then when they lost or they got too far behind, they would start playing, and I'd got probably a couple of lucky shots, and they realised. And next time we played, it was a different game. I had a very good service. I think about 40 per cent of my game was my serve.*

I played once or twice a week in the York League, and playing against a disabled person is different to playing an able bodied person. I could read a table tennis ball in midair so I had a good idea what they were going to do. Facilities-wise there was never

*anywhere to go and there was nobody around really to prac-
tise with in York. Most of my playing was with Yorkshire and
Humberside and a lot of the players came from Lincolnshire.*

Clive moved over into umpiring.

*I umpired at the world championships at Wembley, three
matches a day, and at Birmingham the first event when the
National Exhibition Centre opened. We did the European championships and I was table manager for a while and stood in for
umpiring when they were short. When I umpired, you sat down,
ground level. The only time you stood up was for doubles,
because you can see which side the ball bounced. In service, it's
got to bounce your side and then the opponent's side, and it's
got to go to the right of that white line in the service. The regu-
lations altered a lot. They put an age limit on and I was very
close to that. So the last tournament I umpired was at Selby.*

*You play certain shots because you know your limitations. You
adapt different ways of playing. And the best coach in the world
will not be able to tell you what to do. There are many different
disabled abilities. Like arthritis, how is your hand formed, what
movement have you got? How high can you throw the ball up
for serving and what movement have you got with your shoulders? But when you see people holding a bat in their mouths, it
makes you say, 'What am I grumbling about?'*

*Facilities are getting worse. When I first started, a lot of compa-
nies had a team. Then of course when Mrs Thatcher came in,
they had to nationalise all our assets. Rooms they were playing
in suddenly turned into stockrooms.*

I do go to the York closed [championships] *and I still referee the
matches for them. In York the problem is the officials are getting*

old. They definitely need some younger people to come and start doing some of the work.

I have been passionate about it. To win five national titles in singles and three doubles. I've managed the Yorkshire team at Hull when the manager didn't feel well. I'd already been appointed captain so I took over both roles. I've been chairman, match secretary, press secretary and competitions secretary of the York league.

Clive was given an award for services to table tennis.

— *Chapter 20* —
TAEKWONDO

Taekwondo is a martial art, a form of unarmed combat, its early origins dating back well over 2000 years. In its present form it was founded in 1955, and was established initially for the South Korean military. It appeared first as a demonstration sport in 1988 and 1992, a medal sport in Sydney in 2000, and a Commonwealth Games sport in 2010. It has always been dominated by South Korea, although there was a British gold medallist in the featherweight division in 2000. 'Tae' means to jump, kick or smash with the foot, 'Kwon' means to punch with the fist, and 'Do' is the art.

ALAN SPARKS

Alan Sparks was born in Ireland. He came to Yorkshire in the 1970s where he saw a demonstration of taekwondo. He was very impressed and decided to have a try.

> *I thought it might last a year, but I've been teaching for 30 years. It was the kicking techniques, the modern training techniques, compared to karate and kung fu style, very traditional and not so dynamic. I wanted something a lot more athletic, it impressed me, the power breaking. It isn't just the sports side, that is just temporary. It is the mental training, self defence, and the discipline that goes with it. And that's a lifelong thing. It doesn't matter about age, if you learn to ride a bike or you learn to swim, it stays with you all your life. If you do it for the wrong reasons, you are only getting a fraction of it. You're not getting the full depth, and once you get older and you give up that, you're left with an empty shell. I got more out of it as I progressed.*

Taekwondo group, Alan Sparks is second left at back (Alan Sparks)

Alan was graded to 1st Dan Black Belt in 1983 by Master Rhee Hi Kan who was one of the founders of the sport in Britain in 1967. He then,

trained under Korean master Hee Il Cho and he graded me up to fourth Dan black belt. He's a very famous master. I've a lot of respect for him. He wasn't one of these that put on their uniform and told you what he wanted you to do. I'm a sixth Dan. If I'd stopped in the association, I'd probably be a seventh Dan now and classed as a master. Nine is the top. First, second and third Dans are novice black belts. Fourth, fifth and sixth Dans are classed as experts. Of course it's part of the national curriculum in schools in Korea, just like we have football.

Alan was one of the Global Taekwondo International founder instructors and black belt examiners when it developed from a London-South East based association into a national one. He has competed in national and international events, been a team manager, coach, umpire and referee. He also supported his own children's involvement.

They're 35 and 36 now, they're [part of] a very high level and international team, they've competed abroad, won gold medals and titles.

Alan opened the Alan Sparks Taekwondo School

back in the '80s. I started out at RAF Finningley, then I had classes at Selby. Then I came to York, at Priory Street Community Centre then to the Barbican Centre. I've got three venues

Alan Sparks on far right (Alan Sparks)

*around York that I train at now, Energise, Joseph Rowntree's
School and Haxby Road School. One of my assistant coaches is
a teacher at Malton and she teaches children after school.*

He runs 12 classes a week as well as private tuition, taking classes
personally, but he also has a team of black belt coaches. His training
includes stretching and strengthening exercises, sparring, awareness
and self defence, circuit training and bag work.

*We teach the ITF style [International Taekwondo Federation],
and wear head guard, gloves, safety feet, shin pads and a groin
guard. We make contact but it's light contact, there's boxing
techniques, kicks and punches to the head, everything above the
waist, so it's different styles. [Popularity] goes in waves. The
last real big surge was Bruce Lee in the '70s. That made everyone
want to do martial arts. And then it died down. Then with the
'Karate Kid' film, it came up again, and then Ninja Turtles.*

*It's like an apprenticeship. You start off at Grade 7, work up to
First Cub, that's the black stripe. If you pass the first black belt,
you then go to Dan grades. First to second Dan, it's a minimum
of a year and a half, second to third it's another two years
minimum. Then another three years minimum. I demonstrate
and train with the school. So I'm teaching but I have my work-
outs with them as well, to try and keep fit.*

*I've got around 100 students. I teach at York University as well.
Very occasionally I get someone from beginner to black belt.
I've taught a lot of women self defence over the years, women
who've been in refuges, who've been beaten and things like
that, to bring their confidence up. Self defence is about avoiding
trouble. It's being aware of the environment around you. The
confidence has got to be built inside. As you build your confidence up, you walk in a different manner. If you're going around*

more confident and feeling better about yourself, you're less likely to get picked on. So it's much more than a sport.

Different associations don't bother with the Korean termi-nology but it is part of the traditional training. So you can give instructions in Korean and in English. You learn about the history. There were different umbrella bodies set up. But there's so much politics, it's unbelievable. They used to have the Sports Council, that was a quango, but it's stopped. The main thing is the fact that instructors are qualified and insured. They shouldn't have to be in a particular governing body.

In the competitions,

You might have two or three minute rounds. You get through one round and go on to try somebody different. Initially there might be 32 fighters, and you get down to the quarter finals and so on. We have a matted area about 9 metres square. At one side of the table is a recorder and a timekeeper. At each corner of the square you have a judge with clickers and they score by red or blue tags. When a bout is finished, the referee will shout, 'Show' and they'll show red or blue or a draw, it's done on points. If anybody does excessive contact they get minus points or they get disqualified. There's quite a lot of rules.

Children can begin at about six.

The junior class might be up to the age of 13. They've got to be able to concentrate. We've got health and safety rules all the time. I've got to do risk assessments and go through all the courses. I'm registered with York City Council as a coach. You've got to a proficient level in your martial art, then you've got instructors' courses, coaching courses. We used to go to national

Alan Sparks at his Taekwondo School 2011 (Alan Sparks)

competitions, and my own York championships at the Barbican Centre for a number of years.

I used to do a lot of umpiring and organising competitions, overseeing tournaments and assessing courses. It's not just the competitions where they're fighting or sparring, it's the patterns and forms, doing the set moves. It's the patterns you can win trophies for, as well as the sparring. It is a technique that comes with training. It's smacking and pulling back. In 30 years, I haven't had anybody that's been seriously injured. You might pull a muscle or twist an ankle but I've never had anybody with a tooth knocked out or a broken nose. Risk assessments are done but you are making contact, you can't expect to be wrapped in cotton wool. Rugby and things like that are far more dangerous.

You learn to control your techniques, to produce power. People have got to learn to crawl before they can walk. On grading they do breaking, and break boards and bricks. We're testing people out, checking they've got the control to go on to the next level. It's not just the physical side, but the mental side. I'll assess people and if they're not the right sort of person to teach, I won't teach them. You've got to have the right attitude. If they've got a big ego, they're not going to fit in. They've got to have respect. It's hard work. It's not about fighting, it's self defence, strengthening the body. You can't get results in a few weeks. But you get fitter and more supple.

Chapter 21

TENNIS

Although tennis was contested in 1896, and continued until 1924, it was then dropped for many years. It was a demonstration sport in 1968 and 1984, and returned to the full medal programme in 1988. Great Britain has won 44 medals, (16 gold) which include the indoor tennis contests, no longer part of the Games. The first Olympic title for tennis, in 1896, was won by John Boland of Great Britain and the first woman to win any title in the Olympic Games was an English woman, Charlotte Cooper, who won gold for tennis in 1900.

Tennis has always been a popular sport in York. One of the earliest local clubs was the Grosvenor Lawn Tennis Club which closed in 1916 after thirty years. The 'York Municipal Tournament' of July 1933 included women's singles, women's singles handicap, women's doubles, mixed doubles, men's singles, men's doubles, men's handicap, consolation doubles and girls' singles. York and District Tennis League had three divisions for the first time in 1959. York sportsman Bert Keech, well known particularly for bowls, for which he was a national champion, also rowed for York and played tennis. A municipal tennis tournament in the city was held in his memory in 1955, a year after his death.

Unlike football, historically a working class sport, but becoming popular with the middle classes too, tennis has always had a reputation for being a gentle, genteel, polite sport, played on private courts, accompanied by cucumber sandwiches and Pimm's in the afternoon. But in 2005, the national organisation 'Tennis For Free' was set up to 'address the barriers for participation, and to bring the benefits of playing tennis to as many young people as possible...tennis is a game that can be played by anyone, regardless of ability or social background'. They work with schools and local authorities, to provide free access, coaching and equipment.

York Tennis Club is now based at Clifton Park on Shipton Road, but there are also a number of smaller clubs in the city, which compete as part of The Tyke Petroleum Men's Tennis League, or the York and District Mixed Tennis League, which has eleven divisions. The majority of the clubs are based in local villages like Copmanthorpe, Poppleton and New Earswick. One of the oldest is Fulford Tennis Club, founded in 1949, which has three floodlit tarmac courts and a further five in the adjacent school.

York Tennis Club also plays host to a club called Tennisability, for members with disabilities. They train weekly and put players in to competitions. The club became known through young player, Laura Campbell, who represented Special Olympics Great Britain at the European Summer Games in Warsaw.

MALCOLM HUNTINGTON

The only person in York to have played, umpired and written about a sport, in this case tennis, is Malcolm Huntington, a well-known and popular figure in the city.

I was born in County Durham. I only lived there for about six months then we moved to York. My father Jack Huntington played a little bit for Bishop Auckland [football], which was then a very top amateur team, and was a keen cricketer.

I went to Manor School. My best subject was writing essays. The headmaster said, "It would be nice if you thought of being a journalist when you get to leaving school". He had a word with

Malcolm Huntington, first person in history to umpire three finals - Wimbledon men's final, Olympic final and Davis Cup final (Malcolm Huntington)

the Sports Editor at the Press, Wilf Meek, who covered York City for many years and I got a job there in August 1949 at 15, as a copy boy, running messages, making tea, going to the post office and things like that. But you learnt everything within the building. I stayed until May 1995 when I retired, since when I've continued being a part-time sports writer writing on York City for the Yorkshire Post.

The Yorkshire Evening Press, at its best probably in the '50s, printed 56,000 copies a day, which for 100,000 people, was a phenomenal total. After my training as a 15 year old, I gradually worked my way up to be a junior reporter. I eventually became Deputy Sports Editor, then Sports Editor and then the best job, Chief Sports Writer. That was a very happy time, I was able to go out and meet people and I was very lucky to be voted Yorkshire's Best Sports Writer in '91 and '93. I covered 1,302 York City football matches over the years. When I started, they only covered five sports in any detail, horseracing, football, cricket, rugby union and rugby league. I was determined to broaden the outlook. So I went to every annual meeting and annual dinner, and we were covering about 35 sports by the time I finished. We had a sports paper, initially green. On the day that York City went to the semi final of the FA Cup in March 1955, they sold 25,000 green presses. It became the pink paper because they ran out of green, that finished in 1983.

I was a goalkeeper at school and I played for York City Boys and I got into the Yorkshire Squad and was nominated for the

York Men's Doubles final at York Municipal Tennis Tournament 1959-60, Malcolm Huntington and Derek Robinson (Malcolm Huntington)

*England Schoolboys Team. Then I played for York Railway
Institute in a minor league football as a goalkeeper. But I had to
give up Saturday afternoon sport to work in the office. I played
a lot of cricket, I was York junior table tennis champion, I took
up squash, then later in life badminton and golf. Now I play
golf, tennis and swim a lot.*

*I grew up next to Rowntree's Park and I learnt to play tennis
there. When I was 22, I won the York men's singles title. And
later won the mixed doubles with my wife. She played for
Yorkshire and she's played at Wimbledon. I got started as an
umpire because I played in a tournament in Ilkley in 1959, and
everybody who lost a match, umpired one of the matches. I
was sitting on the high chair keeping the score, and I became
aware of an old gentleman, Johnny Heron. He said, "Have you
ever thought of becoming an umpire?" "No. I'm only umpiring
here because I lost a match". "I've been watching you and I
think you've got some idea of what's going on, so will you give
it a try?" He pulled out an application form to join the Lawn
Tennis Advisors' Association, persuaded me to fill this in, the
following year I was at Wimbledon. I had 36 years of umpiring.
I started on court 16 the furthermost court, and eventually I
umpired at six finals on Centre Court, at the Olympic Games
twice and two Davis Cup finals, and about 14 or 15 Davis Cups
all over the world.*

*In 1960 the big players were Neale Fraser, the Australian, the
first men's singles champion I saw, Rod Laver, the best player
I ever umpired. And then people like Pancho Gonzalez, Lew
Hoad, Ilie Nastase, Ken Rosewall, Boris Becker and, among
the women, Billie Jean King, Steffi Graf, Martina Navratilova,
Chris Lloyd. It's been a wonderful journey, to umpire all the
best players in the world. McEnroe, a very brash New York kid,
came to the fore at Wimbledon, a marvellous feat when you're*

an up and coming. *Of course his conduct then was reprehensible. I'd umpired him on 11 or 12 occasions and I only had trouble with him once, he said to me, "For a guy who can't add two plus two, you're doing a wonderful job". It wasn't anything I'd done wrong, the outburst was because he was foot faulted and he wouldn't believe it. The referee Alan Mills got his father to go and sit behind the line judge and prove he was foot faulting.*

Malcolm Huntington, umpire, and John McEnroe, Wimbledon 1980s (Malcolm Huntington)

And from that day to this, he's never foot faulted. Nastase was more fun. When it was raining he used to borrow somebody's umbrella and try to play with one hand, or hide under the stop net. He was a great character. But it was part of the learning curve. When you get to the top of the tree, being on the Davis Cup panel, you were expected to take the trials of a tennis match. They virtually rewrote the rules, and a succession of penalties. Now umpires know exactly where they stand.

But McEnroe has another side to him. Simon Hoare was a player in the '70s and his hero was McEnroe. Sadly Simon was in a crash and had severe brain injuries. We went to visit him in hospital, he was in a coma for about three months. And his father Terry got in touch with McEnroe. And McEnroe made a tape, "Come on Simon, this is John McEnroe, I hear you've been in an accident. Don't give up, and battle on". His father played this tape to him dozens and dozens of times and he gradually started to emerge from the coma. And that's the side of McEnroe that nobody will ever see. He used to give a lot of money to charity and help people in that way, and he has become a wonderful commentator, what I call a poacher turned game-keeper.

Malcolm was the first person to umpire the three major finals, the men's singles at Wimbledon, the women's Olympic final in Los Angeles, and two Davis Cup finals.

I actually stopped umpiring in 1992 at Wimbledon, I decided that I didn't want to go downhill. The last match was on Centre Court, Newcombe and Roche, the very famous pair, versus Reece and Stewart in the over 45 finals. After that I did about three years as a linesman, a team leader helping youngsters.

I used to use part of my holiday which was then five weeks.

What I did then couldn't be achieved now because the top umpires now are professionals, full-time. When I went to Wimbledon in 1960, the players were amateur. Neale Fraser, the champion, got a £25 voucher and expenses. We got a free lunch, a free tea, second class rail fare from York to Wimbledon, and the ability to buy at face value six pairs of centre court tickets, five pairs for court 1. Now an umpire of standing would get £3000, and any expenses. And the winner of Wimbledon gets £1.1 million.

My record was six hours 35 minutes to umpire a match, which is a long long time. I've done that once at Wimbledon, once at a Davis Cup final in Frankfurt. And I finished up having my dinner at 11 o'clock at night.

Malcolm got the MBE for 'services to Yorkshire sports journalism'.

In my time, you started at 15 and retired at 65. I was given the opportunity to go to a national, to Manchester. I decided that I wanted to be in York, I knew a lot of people and they knew me, so I was able to get stories.

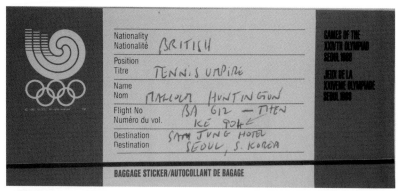

Seoul Olympics 1988, baggage sticker for umpire Malcolm Huntington (Malcolm Huntington)

In 1984 tennis was brought back into the Olympic Games in Los Angeles. I was appointed chief umpire for the tennis demonstration event. I umpired a ladies' final and when I came back, I said, "I've just seen one of the best players I've ever seen, a little girl called Steffi Graf", who was then 15. "Never heard of her". I said, "Well you will do". She won Wimbledon seven times. The next time I umpired her was my last major final in 1988, when she beat Martina Navratilova to win her first Wimbledon title. The men's singles title was also won by an unheard of player, Stefan Edberg. In 1988, I was lucky enough to be selected for Seoul. At Wimbledon I suppose you might do 15-20 matches if you're at top level, sometimes two a day. At the Olympics you did six or seven, but they're all the best umpires in the world and you wouldn't expect any more than that.

Wimbledon 1988 Malcolm Huntington and Steffi Graf at women's final (Malcolm Huntington)

As an umpire you are discouraged from being friendly with the players. I was umpiring in Bangkok, and I was standing next to Vijay Amritraj, the great Indian player, and he had some lovely gold rings and bangles. And I was admiring these, and he said, "I was in so-and-so country and I bought that". Later that night the referee, Fred Hoyle, came up to me, "Malcolm, we've had a complaint that you were seen talking to Amritraj, from Mark Edmondson", who was a very tough Australian character. This fellow thought I might have been cooking something up because he might have been playing in the next round. You tend to keep apart from the players. You're friendly, "Good morning", and that, but they don't want to talk to you and you don't want to talk to them.

I used to line judge as well as umpire. Line judges are extremely important. They can cripple you if they take bad decisions and you have to overrule or try to. Of course they've now got

York officials at Wimbledon c1990, Malcolm Huntington, (umpire) Christine Place, John Linfoot and Victor Fielder line judges (Malcolm Huntington)

Hawkeye. If a ball's flashing past you at 120 miles an hour, at best it's a guesstimate. The most important thing in any sport is trying to come to the right decision by whatever means you can. And that must include technology.

It took me from 1960 to about '76 to umpire a match on centre court at Wimbledon. People notice you and decide whether you're good enough to get into the C grade, B grade and then eventually A1. Then I got on the International Panel which were officials. The Davis Cup, we've got to have neutral officials that can overrule the linesman. I was one of the six selected from Britain, there were six from France, Germany and America. I went on to umpiring Sweden, Ireland, Sicily, Czechoslovakia, Soviet Union, Australia, America, and had a marvellous time meeting a lot of people all over the world. I was very fortunate I was able to do something I enjoyed, both in my leisure time and my work time. That has brought me a lot of happiness and contentment.

JOHN LINFOOT

John Linfoot, though born in Manchester, has spent most of his life in York.

I've played tennis all my life and have been chairman of York Tennis Club for the last 25 years. My first club was Rowntree Park. I played many a happy hour then. Rowntree's had three of the best tennis courts in York [on Haxby Road at the factory]. *Then they were wanted for car parking space and we had to move out to Mille Crux further down the road. Then they became hard courts which are still there.*

In 1966 Tang Hall Tennis Club, which I was a member of, was given notice to quit. This coincided with a club called Sycamore, who played in Water Lane on the site of the YWCA, also having to move, so we joined them to play on the courts in Water Lane as Clifton Tennis Club. The following year we approached York Cricket Club who had moved from Wigginton Road to the new site, Clifton Park, on Shipton Road. We became York Tennis Club, playing on three shale courts in 1967. We now have six courts, five are astro turf and one is a carpet court, they are considered to be the best in York. We've got 16 competitive sides in various leagues. There's the York and District mixed tennis leagues, one of the biggest mixed leagues in the country with 88 teams, and 11 divisions. There's a local ladies league, a local mens' doubles league, we've got mixed teams and a veteran's team. Wednesday evenings and Saturday afternoon sessions are very popular. Once the season starts, the match players tend not to come down then because they're too busy with other matches.

We've got a flourishing junior section of about 100 members, from about five or six up to 15 or 16. We've got a flourishing day membership of housewives and retirees. The surface is so user friendly, people are playing well into the 70s. If it was tarmac I don't think they would still be playing.

I was a Wimbledon umpire for 26 years, from '76 to 2001, and I used to umpire local tennis tournaments. I was on several finals as a linesperson but I've never umpired a final. I was faced with a choice, did I want to go up to the next grade or not, and because I had a young family and a fulltime job, to maintain a higher standard I'd have to do far more umpiring on a local level and I just couldn't afford the time.

My grade was sufficiently good enough to get me on the show courts as a linesman. Malcolm Huntington was my mentor really, he got me interested in going to Wimbledon. You'd go to a hatch and get your instructions for the day, you were assigned to one court. I got this piece of paper saying, 'Please umpire the third match on court 12', you can imagine how daunting that was, your first Wimbledon, and you are umpiring a championship match, which would never happen nowadays because you've got to go through training courses.

The first Wimbledon I remember was the very hot summer of 1976, and Bjorn Borg won the championships. The pinnacle was in 1991 when I was on the men's finals both years, Edberg and Becker. And I was also in a final for Steffi Graf.

Malcolm was high up in the hierarchy and obviously if he recommended somebody, they would know that this person was fairly competent. I got through it okay. I was conscious of other umpires hovering round making notes. Afterwards you come down from the chair, get taken for a cup of tea and a debrief. Shortly afterwards I got a letter to say I'd been accepted as a full member. Now you never get to umpire championship matches unless you're a white badge or a gold badge or whatever, which is probably how it should be.

On the first Tuesday lunchtime was the umpire's cocktail party, and play would start at two o'clock and everybody turned up on the lawn. And they're sipping these drinks, it's red hot and I'm thinking it's a bit dodgy. Not surprisingly at half past two a poor old lady, [line judge] fell asleep. After three or four years, they changed to the evening. There's always an upsurge in tennis around Wimbledon time, at the club. People want to play more. If you went to Wimbledon it was the icing on the cake as far as officials were concerned. It paid for my family's annual holiday.

I am a qualified elementary coach as well. In the summer we've got a timetable of events and we also hire the courts to St Peter's School. The Lawn Tennis Association is working very hard to promote tennis at grass roots level. If you look in the top hundred of tennis, we maybe have one person. The LTA are trying through schools partnerships and satellite clubs to get more playing. Being affiliated to the county association enables clubs to obtain interest free loans which we've made use of once or twice. And there's technical support, if you wanted flood-lights or anything. Coaching isn't cheap but a decent racquet's not pricy and our junior membership is £25 for a year. A lot depends on how much the schools push tennis. You've got to have children playing regular tennis, coach tournaments. It's not an easy thing to achieve.

— *Chapter 22* —

VOLLEYBALL

Volleyball, beach volleyball and handball are all Olympic sports, but only volleyball is played in the city of York. Beach volleyball is relatively new, and only became a medal sport in 1996. Handball was introduced in the 1936 games but then there was a 12 year gap. Britain has never entered a team but will do so in 2012. Volleyball first began in the USA in 1895 and became an Olympic sport in 1964. Britain has never won any medals in any of the three sports.

A York Youth Volleyball Club started in 1972 at St George's School in Margaret Street, but the York Volleyball Club was started by Peter Bibby in 1974. It still continues today, at Huntington School, York College and the Energise centre. The club holds an annual outdoor tournament, the VolleyFest, and also includes some beach volleyball in Bridlington and Whitby. The Club is fourth in the Mens' National League Division in 2012.

PETER BIBBY

Although he was born in Upton in the Wirral in 1947, Peter Bibby has spent most of his life in York. He trained in PE and geography in London, and started playing volleyball in 1966. In 1969 he was selected for the England squad and came to teach at Nunthorpe Grammar School in York.

As a PE teacher you cover a wide variety of things. In winter months we had football and rugby. Steve McClaren [England manager 2006–7] *was at the school. He wasn't just a good footballer but a great all-round performer. In the summer months*

Nunthorpe Grammar School boys gymnastics display on Knavesmire with HM The Queen 1971, Pete Bibby in tracksuit next to gymnast (Pete Bibby)

you had cricket, tennis and athletics. In the later years we did hockey and basketball. I was trying to introduce volleyball, it was a slow process.

There was so much going on in my life. I was teaching and I did five lunchtimes and five evenings a week [with Nunthorpe] *and then Saturdays. Sundays were generally free of school commitments but that was the day for playing volleyball.*

Volleyball in this country started very much with the Polish airmen just after the war, particularly in the Midlands. They had their own particular style of playing. The England team was a real minnow in the world. In 1969 at Crystal Palace in London, there was a small tournament arranged and we played against Japan and Czechoslovakia, the top Eastern European team. To have that opportunity was really super. Japan had

*won the silver medal at the '68 Mexico Olympics and gold
medal in '72, so we were playing a top world nation.*

*They gave us a demonstration of a training session for the
Japanese. It was awe-inspiring. They were selected for their
height and agility. Then they were taught the game of volleyball
and that proved to be an absolute masterstroke. You do need an
awful lot of agility. I was a setter, I wasn't really tall enough
to be a smasher, or a spiker. My expertise was the agility on the
back court, diving, picking up the ball. I always used to damage
my hip bone and I'd wear a dense foam pad in there. You moved
around the positions but you could learn to protect the smaller
people. I was just about six foot. There was a seven foot one
Israeli* [volleyball player], *and the Belgians were six foot eight
and six foot eleven. They spar up above the net, you get four
arms and legs, like a set of windscreen wipers. The ball disap-
pears back down your own throat.*

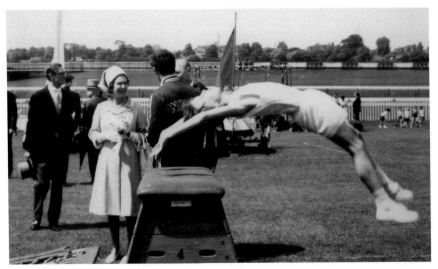

*Nunthorpe Grammar School boys gymnastic display 1971, Pete Bibby in tracksuit talking
to HM The Queen. (Pete Bibby)*

To play the game you need flexibility, an eye for a ball, and you do have to work hard on your leg muscles because of the constant jumping for smashing or blocking. We did a lot of measuring with the sergeant jump, your standing jump, to improve that. It wasn't as if today, with football, you kick a tin can from the age of three, I didn't pick the game up until much later in life.

To get to the Olympics, you'd have had to win, or been very strongly placed, in the full European championships, because they can only take in a certain number of teams. We were lucky to win one or two matches in the Western European tournament, never mind the full European tournament and finishing near the top.

My first international [with England] was against Scotland, in Edinburgh. It was a nice experience to get there. The following April I'd been selected for the Great Britain squad to go to Finland [in 1969]. That was the West European tournament and we played eight matches. I was doing a lot of riding of the bench but it was all getting experience. There was 12 in the squad, only six on court.

As with all amateur sports, Pete had to pay his own expenses when he travelled.

When I went to Finland I was asked to pay £48 and my dad said, "I'm not going to let money get in the way of your first international cap". Every year for the first few years, I was having to pay some contribution for the big tournaments, for accommodation and air fare and training. It wasn't an easy time.

In England, volleyball was normally played inside.

We did go to Holland to a big outdoor tournament. That was a tremendous experience, we had wonderful weather. Just field after field after field with volleyball courts. There wasn't much structure for outdoor volleyball in this country. Whenever you did find it, they were hard courts.

When the York club started,

John Hutt was head of PE at St Peter's and was very helpful in getting us in there. They had a lovely sports hall. I really wanted that club started because if I was teaching the boys at

Pete Bibby on right playing volleyball c1973 (Pete Bibby)

Nunthorpe to play the game, and we played wherever we could, often against senior teams, there's got to be some progression once they do leave school. We had to pay a subscription for the hire of the facilities. All they provided was a set of posts which were initially weighted down. I did finally persuade them to get some proper posts sunk into the ground. I used to take nets and two dozen balls. At the time I was playing for them, and coach, referee, secretary, fixtures secretary, treasurer, you name it. We very quickly opened it to men and women. I wanted to improve that side. They were a lovely bunch of people. It was probably 7 to 9pm, and then we'd retire to the Burton Stone Lane pub for a quick shandy. We'd compete mainly against teams in the Yorkshire area. I remember playing at the US airbase, Menwith Hill, one year. That was fantastic.

Pete Bibby with England squad 1974, (in centre in tracksuit). Pete got 38 caps for England, 8 for Great Britain (Pete Bibby)

*Great Britain volleyball squad
badge and
England volleyball squad badge*
(Pete Bibby)

*There was a little bit going with York University. I think I did
coach them for a while. A guy called John Blackburn ran the
volleyball club and he asked me to do some coaching. But I was
also involved in the Centre of Excellence at Carnegie College in
Leeds.*

*We did have quite a number of trips to Sweden and Denmark.
But the major tournaments were Finland then Israel 1970, which
was very interesting indeed close to the Lebanese border. '71
was Sweden, '72 was Greece, '73 should have been that bigger
tournament in Italy but that was aborted. '74 was Turkey. Then
in '75 I was coaching a side in Paris for the West European
tournament. I took a qualification, the International Volleyball
Coaches Award. That was ten days, based in Loughborough, a
fantastic course.*

I was training with the England squad until 1975, by which time I was also a staff referee and a staff coach. I was running weekend courses and did a summer school in Exeter.

Of course volleyball was a demanding game,

especially on the knees and hips. You had to stay as fit as you could. People think the PE teacher is a pretty fit person, that's a bit of a misnomer, because you are trotting around refereeing, a quick sprint here and there, but you're not really training physically hard. You have to do that in your own time. And finding the time for that was quite difficult.

Eventually Pete had to make a choice, and he continued to coach alongside his work in school.

The refereeing side I took on more myself. My lifetime pattern – you play as long as you can, whilst the ideas are fresh in your mind, when you finish playing you become a coach, unless you really work hard at staying at the top. You'll eventually become out of date as a coach. So then you become a referee. You've got a lifetime experience of playing and coaching. When your eyesight fails you become an official, an administrator. And then there's only one place to go, in a wooden box, the four stages of life.

I carried on till 1983 with York Volleyball Club, still doing lots of coaching but by that time I was also starting to become heavily involved with rugby. I still love the game, it gave me so much but I couldn't have become a fulltime volleyball coach, I've got too many interests in other sports. I just love to impart my enthusiasm for other games.

To have a variety of sports that children can do and adults can support as well, is good. The amount of money in football you might say is a little bit obscene and you have to question how long that can last. It's always going to be the case that certain sports dominate. Places like Cuba who are very strong in certain traditions, have a very good volleyball team, very good at boxing, they just concentrate on a small number of sports. You might say the same of Jamaica, cricket and athletics. The fairness of the British, they will try to some extent to cover every sport and with a population of nearly 70 million, there's probably enough people to play these sports but they can't all have the standing of football or rugby.

What is the driving force in sport? You need to be single minded. If the opposition is better than you, you need to learn from that. Winning has never been my philosophy. I'm a technician rather than a tactician. Enjoyment is the number one thing.

When I came to York, we still had the cattle market where the Barbican is, and it was mooted back in the early '70s that Shepherd's were going to build a community sports hall for £500,000. About 12 years later it still hadn't been built and the cost was about £8 million or something. York is ideally situated to stage international matches. They should have had an international class swimming pool because it's always had a tradition in swimming. They could host anything, because it's got the transport links, it's got accommodation, it's got the historical aspects.

The rewards that York would get back from the tourism industry, international teams wanting to play for York, would put York up there on a pedestal.

— Chapter 23 —
WATER POLO

The sport of water polo dates back to the 19th century, and is one of the few Olympic sports to originate in Great Britain. It was among the first team sports in the Olympic Games in 1900, though women's teams only began to compete in 2000. Britain won gold medals in 1900, 1908, 1912 and 1920.

DENNIS WOODCOCK

Dennis Woodcock was born in York in 1933. His first interest was in swimming and he swam for York, and later Yorkshire. He began to play water polo in 1947, and had four years playing for Yorkshire in the late 1950s.

Brian Durkin and I were the youngest ones ever to play, and we played for York City at 14. There was a chap called George Lester, a good player and a good teacher. We had training sessions in the river, at the back of Bootham School. I got involved with York City River Swimming Club, then York City Baths Club. And that's where I started playing water polo properly.

It was a minor sport then, and amateur. You paid all your own expenses, right down to petrol money going to Galashiels when we got drawn in the big cup. We got in the York team because we were fast swimmers. There were seven in the team, including the centre forward, centre half, two fullbacks and a goalie. The referee used to throw the ball in the middle of the pool and each team had to race to get the ball, then you flipped it back to your team. You can only touch it with one hand at a time. And you

Dennis Woodcock, Brian Durkin, Derek Stubbs, Rowntree's Park c1952

(Dennis Woodcock)

can't stand. The rules have changed enormously over the years. I finished playing when I was 52. We played once a week or once a fortnight, home and away. There was about 15 teams in the Yorkshire league. We won the Yorkshire championship once at Bradford. We played in 1951 for the Festival of Britain, at the bottom of St Mary's, where people could watch. We had a lot of people from York and a few from Halifax. My father was refereeing, in a boat on the halfway line. We won of course. All the York swimmers said, "We're going to get Mr Woodcock and duck him". And they swam to the boat and tipped it up. My dad was in his best blazer and everything. All he could say was, "I've got my teeth in". He didn't want to lose his teeth in the river.

In the deep end in a swimming pool you couldn't stand. In the shallow end you used to keep right down low and your feet on the bottom as though you weren't standing. But any movement that looked as though you'd jumped off the bottom, the referee would blow the whistle and give a foul to the other side. When the rules changed, they blew the whistle for a foul and you could still move around. They brought the rule in, after I'd finished, where they had to have cups over their ears, because you could get a blow on the ear if you were going for the ball and missed it.

Rowntree's Gala at Yearsley pool. Dennis Woodcock 2nd right at back

(Dennis Woodcock)

In some places they had floating goals. And others were brought out and fixed on the end of the pool by brackets that someone had made. The height was different at each end because it was lower in the deep end and higher in the shallow end, you could only jump and save there. You had to kick in the deep end to try and get up.

The floating goals were the same height, three foot from the water, and 25 yards pitch. We had to keep the goalposts up to date and service them. We played up at Galashiels and got knocked out of the cup, (like the FA cup), where you get drawn against anyone, national league. We did go on a tour around Cheltenham, Gloucester, Bristol. They were the very best at water polo, we got a real thrashing because the standard was so high.

The team finished up playing at St John's swimming pool. Prior to that we used to play in the big pool at Yearsley, the biggest pitch you could get for polo. The other teams didn't like coming there because there was too much swimming. When you're in the smaller pools, you don't swim too much. We had a good player called Peter Kendrew who is still swimming today. He was an international swimmer but also a good water polo player, and he was left handed. There weren't many of them around so they used to put him on the left wing and he'd swim up there and could use his left hand very good.

There were terrible fouls under the water. I used to go through three or four swimming costumes a year, getting them pulled off, you got lots of kicks. We went to play once at Dawdon Colliery up at Newcastle. That was 30 foot deep all over. The lining of their pool had been painted black and it looked like black water. You couldn't stand there at all. The referee was on a one metre diving board. We could hardly throw the ball up to him because it was so tight and not being able to stand, we were out of our depth!! If there was a foul and they needed to send you off, you got sent off until there was another score and you came back.

The original ball they used was leather, which absorbed water, and then became heavier,

The size of a football with small panels. But they brought the other one out with rough dimples, so you get a grip. When they were fresh, the new type of ball was really good.

Everybody had either a white cap or a blue cap so the referee could distinguish which team was which. They were numbered from one to seven, so you could say, "Number two come here". He wouldn't know individual names. The goalies had red caps on.

York Water Polo Club continues today at Energise Centre. Members have to be at least eight years old and be able to swim 50 metres. The University of York Swimming and Water Polo Club is very active in competitions, and is based at Archbishop Holgate's School.

— Chapter 24 —
WEIGHTLIFTING

Weightlifting in England is regulated by the British Weightlifting Association, but there are also regional squads. In September 2011, British Weightlifting held its centenary celebrations in York, an event which attracted weightlifters from all over the UK. Former Olympians and commonwealth lifters were also celebrated at the event, which consisted of a day of weightlifting at York University Sports Centre followed by an evening banquet.

Olympic weightlifting consists of a lift with a barbell weighing 20 kilos, which is loaded with weight plates at either end. Competitors are in categories of age and body weight. Men's weightlifting has been an Olympic sport since 1896, but women's weightlifting has only been contested since 2000. The men's competition has been dominated by Russia and the USA.

BRYN JONES

Bryn Jones was born in Scarborough and came to York in 1980 to attend St John's College, where he studied leisure management and PE. He went on to do a PGCE at the Carnegie Centre in Leeds. He has been interested in weight training since the age of 16.

So I did the British Weightlifting Association Instructors' course. When I left college and started working, I found myself getting involved in a weightlifting club in York, at Priory Street Community Centre. That was the first and only Olympic weightlifting club in York. We had one or two England juniors and England school boy champions. We had a good thriving little club. Olympic weightlifting is completely different to weight training or body building or power lifting or 'strong man'. Anybody can do it, any age, you don't have to be big, whatever shape, it doesn't make any difference. It's good exercise.

You've got two lifts to do, one is the 'clean and jerk', and the other is called the 'snatch'. In a competition you have three attempts at each. The total of your best snatch and your best clean and jerk gives you your overall competition total. You're lifting body weight categories so, like boxing, it's lightweight, heavyweight, middle weight, bantam weight. It's very fast, very technical, very explosive and very athletic. It's a good sport to watch done well. They say it's the fastest movement of an Olympic sport.

The challenge of Olympic lifting, it's so good for the core structure of the body, it's great for your legs, your back, every part of your body, great for building strength and just getting into better shape. If you technically get it right, it's one of the best feelings in the world. It's a natural high.

The Priory Street Sports and Community Centre closed in the 1990s. Although there are many gyms and centres concentrating on fitness and body building, the only place in York which offers Olympic weightlifting is the David Lloyd Leisure Centre on Hull Road where Bryn lifts and coaches.

You need the proper Eleiko weightlifting bars which are highly sprung, expensive bars. Because you're lifting weights overhead, you're dropping the weight, so it's got to be on a properly built

Bryn Jones weightlifting at David Lloyd Gym, York 2011 (Van Wilson)

platform which can take the weight. It's a really nice set up for it. What's really important is to be coached properly. You can have kids from 9, 10, 11 years old. They can compete. We're very careful with the weights they do. The important thing is to get the lifts right technically so we're not trying to push them to huge amounts of weight. Then from 16 onwards, they are starting to get pretty competitive and they're very strong. You can go right through the age groups. We have people 80 plus. And there's a lot more women getting involved. It is not only a great sport itself but an integral part as assistance for other sports. Quite often I find myself coaching rugby league players

*or rowers or athletes who want to get that bit of explosive
power or speed off the mark.*

*People can do it recreationally but like any other sport, the
more you do it, the better you tend to get. For a lot of athletes,
they might use the Olympic lifts during their winter training, to
build up their explosive strength and power for the start of the
season in summer.*

*I went to America, did my Master's there and I used to teach in
the PE programme. I was the advanced weights trainer back in
the '80s. It was interesting to watch the American footballers
at college, they are so incredibly strong. At that time in this
country, you'd very rarely see any rugby players doing the
Olympic lifts, particularly the 'power clean', which is relevant
to so many sports. Now I think people have realised how they
should incorporate this into their training. If you have that bit
more explosive power and speed, that slight edge, that could
be enough between success and failure. The beauty of Olympic
weightlifting, it's not about becoming big and bulky, it's about
building your core strength. One of the reasons why it is a
minority sport, besides access facilities, is it's not easy and it's
a very technical thing. It's hard work. But it's a great sport.
When I was in the American university, the football team had
a 40,000 seat stadium and down the road at a much bigger
university, Ohio State, they had a 110,000 seat stadium. That is
a different scale. The money that goes into it is at a completely
different level. A lot of people there go to compete at sports
through university, they get scholarships if they are talented.*

*In the past it's not really tried to appeal here. Now the Weight-
lifting Association is trying to build a wider audience. And
there are more school boys and girls, some really talented
athletes. It's great to see them enjoying it and taking a lot of*

pride in it. The only problem is, it is largely run by volunteers. You are relying on people's goodwill and time. People give a lot of their time for free, as with a lot of sports, week in and week out, running these clubs.

It was in the '90s that the British became more aware of the positive benefits of weightlifting. Bryn was chairman of the North of England Weightlifting Association until August 2010, when he had to stand down through lack of time.

We tried to make the competitions much more engaging and exciting. A lot of it is how the sport is presented, how events are presented so they motivate the athletes and the audience really enjoy coming to the event, and make it a bit of a spectacle. If you can see some reward for it, it all helps. In some countries they are sponsored by the state. I think some sports are better at lobbying at a national level to get more funding. It needs to be more proficient in attracting more funding to help the sport develop.

Weightlifting categories range from 56kg to over 105kg. Bryn came fifth in the 85kg class of the 2008 World Masters Weightlifting Championships in Kefalonia, Greece, competing against participants from all over the world. In February 2010, he won the 'Best Lifter' award at the Northern Masters championships.

To help itself, the sport needs to have regional squads, that are open to anybody in the region. As long as they are a member of the British Weightlifting Association, for insurance benefits as well as anything, they get coached by top regional coaches.

I'll be very surprised if we have any athletes who will challenge for a medal in 2012. The standards are so high. And weightlifting in this country has got so far to go to reach that standard. *But we produce athletes that win the Commonwealth Games, win youth titles at commonwealth level, and maybe certain European levels as well.*

When I was in London I used to train with Delroy McQueen who did win the Commonwealth Games, but that was his life for four years, and absolutely nothing else, to win the commonwealth gold. He was outstanding but it was a huge commitment. There is a big price. And when you go to America and see the resources they have, it makes you realise how up against it we are. It's totally another world. But it's a lot better in this country than it was.

We're here about three times a week. We lift and we'll coach as well. I love it, it's the adrenalin and we get a lot of good fun out of it. There's a huge amount of camaraderie. Everybody knows everybody and everybody is very supportive of each other. People have made lifelong friendships from it. There are a lot of talented people, committed people, giving their time to weightlifting. I hope, beyond the Olympics, that the momentum isn't lost.

— *Chapter 25* —
WRESTLING

Wrestling is one of the oldest types of combat, and there are two styles in the Olympic Games, Freestyle and Greco-Roman. The former allows the use of legs in both offence and defence, and has appeared at every Games since 1904. Greco-Roman (a sport for men only) has been contested since 1908. The categories range from heavyweight, which can be over 100kg, down to middleweight, welterweight, lightweight, featherweight, bantamweight and flyweight which is up to 52kg.

Ken Richmond, the British heavyweight, won a bronze medal at the 1952 Games in Helsinki. He was one of the three men who beat the giant gong at the start of J Arthur Rank films. He revealed, however, in 2006, that the huge gong was actually made of papier maché, as the sound would have been deafening for the person banging it.

The first performance of all- in wrestling at the Exhibition Buildings in York took place in February 1933. In 1937, Eddie Philips fought in York, the first time that a reigning champion had appeared. York became a popular venue, particularly in the 1950s and 1960s, for wrestling as entertainment. Contests were held in the Drill Hall, Colliergate and later the SS Empire in Clifford Street, which is now the Grand Opera House, and was known for its live wrestling shows. The sport was first televised from there in 1958.

ARTHUR THOMPSON

Olympic wrestling, however, is an amateur sport. The only known York wrestler to take part in the Olympic Games is Arthur Thompson. He was born in 1911, was a charge-hand bricklayer with the main-

It's How You Play The Game

tenance department at Rowntree's, and died in 1978. He competed in the Olympics in Berlin in 1936 in the men's lightweight freestyle category. The Evening Press reported him as saying,

> *We marched right past Hitler at the opening and closing ceremonies but I didn't pay much attention. When you go there, all you concentrate on is the sport. I spent the time training or wrestling. The British team was given very good treatment. If you were wearing official costume, you could get free transport and go to theatres without paying. Accommodation was excellent.*

During the war Arthur was a PT instructor in the army in Lincoln. When he retired from Rowntree's after 39 years, in 1976, he still held the record for being British lightweight champion in eight consecutive years, 1933 to 1940.

JOHN COX

In more recent times, York's John Cox is the most well-known York wrestler, though he was a professional. He took a ten year break from his career in the ambulance service and wrestled in many national and international tournaments, including those in Germany, Greece, and Beirut in 1967. He became interested, after being a first aid volunteer at the Empire shows. His debut came in October 1962 against fellow Yorkshireman Jim Armstrong. In the 1970s he returned to ambulance driving but continued to wrestle part time. After retirement, he became a popular after dinner speaker, recounting his many experiences in the sport.

RICHARD FOWLER

Frank Richard Fowler, known as Richard, son of the boxer Frank Fowler, was well-known as a boxer and rugby player, but he also did some wrestling.

There was more boxing in the 1920s in York than wrestling. But there were some quite good amateur wrestling clubs. I knew an old chap who represented England, Arthur Thompson, he was a fantastic fellow. He was really pleased when he knew I was doing some wrestling. I used to go to a place near Barnsley to train, the Old White Bear. One or two old wrestling guys would take us there, show us how to wrestle.

Richard Fowler (in centre) wrestling in Beirut 1965. Guards had to escort the competitors out. (Richard Fowler)

Purely amateur wrestling is a bit boring, it's not a great spec-tator sport. There's a lot more showmanship in professional wrestling. I used to work up in Edinburgh and Glasgow, or down in Nottingham. But I'd do it so we got holidays abroad. I went to Spain and then the Canary Islands. I also went to the Middle East, Beirut, and Egypt and that area. Beirut was the Mecca for the rich Arabs, every night you used to get invites after the wrestling to go to the embassy parties. They got guys from all over the world, Russian, Italian, Spanish, Mexican, American. Some of them had been very good wrestlers, some of them were Olympic wrestlers, like the Hungarians. We used to wrestle against the Arabs. They had their own champions. The Saudi princes would gamble on it.

— Chapter 26 —
SPORTS SHOPS

York has had its share of sports shops in the city. Guy Mitchell was born in 1931 and came to York when he was six.

My father [Thomas Mitchell] *was a professional footballer in Newcastle and Leeds. It started with a family dream during the war and my father was then manager of York City* [from 1936 to 1950, joining the Board of Directors from 1961 to 1969]. *He volunteered for the RAF and talked about having a sports shop after the war. I went into Newitt's, the big sports shop, for three years. We opened the first shop in 1950, now part of the Grange Hotel in Bootham. My father had connections, there were army units around York, and schools, he went round and brought business to us and I managed the shop. Then we moved into Church Street and the business took off.*

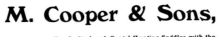

M. Cooper & Sons,

Established 1851.

Seven First Prize Medals Awarded

For Ladies' and Gents' Hunting Saddles with the Open Gullet Ventilation, first brought out by the late MR. M. COOPER, over 45 years ago, and are Noted for Ease, Comfort, and Durability.

Patronised
— by —
Royalty.

DRESS SUIT CASES
DRESS BASKETS
OVERLAND TRUNKS
HAND BAGS
HAT CASES, &c.

HUNTING and
DRIVING WHIPS,
BITS,
SPURS,
FLASKS,
SANDWICH CASES.

COOPER'S CELEBRATED RIBBLESDALE "KIT" BAG.

Pair Horse and Single Harness, Horse Clothing, Hunting and Riding Bridles, and all Stable Requisites.

Note Address:— **4 and 6, Railway Street, YORK.**

Advertisement for Cooper's sports shop

There were two real sports shops. Robson and Cooper were a travel shop, with sports as a sideline, and Hooks in Coppergate were mainly guns and fishing. We sold sports equipment, footwear and clothing, years later it became a fashion trade. When

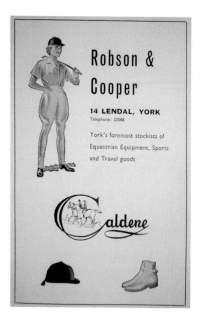

we started there wasn't much in clothing, apart from fleecy tracksuits, rugby and football shirts. There was no such thing as running shoes, now very common. You still had clothing coupons, and football clubs had to keep coupons to buy a set of strips.

We did a lot of club and school business. In 1968 we bought the property at 1 and 2 Colliergate. I was on five committees at one time. So I knew what the players wanted. I played badminton, tennis, table tennis. I supplied a lot of gear to York Fencing Club. We did swimwear and goggles, and a lot of bowls, none of the other shops did it at the time. We had a tremendous run on snooker for a period and an unbelievable one on darts.

In the mid '60s and '70s, more people wanted to play sport and to get fit. They had more money and leisure time. But it was the fashion side that took off.

EPILOGUE

This book is a celebration of the commitment and dedication of York athletes in Olympic sports. One of the key things which emerges from these stories is the importance of coaches and other volunteers, including successful athletes who have themselves gone on to train others to give something back. Without the huge amount of time given by them, unpaid and often unsung, as they encouraged others in the pursuit of excellence, goals could not have been reached or medals won.

Over the door to the players' entrance at Wimbledon are the lines from the Kipling poem, 'If', 'If you can meet with Triumph and Disaster and treat those two impostors just the same', illustrating the point that part of sport is learning to lose with dignity. Many people believe that the sheer enjoyment of taking part, and learning teamwork, should be the motivation, in the words of American sportswriter, Grantland Rice, 'It isn't whether you win or lose, but it's how you play the game'.

This book is dedicated to all those who have excelled in sport in our city, and those who have, behind the scenes, helped them. Both are an inspiration to us and a model to our young people.

As this book goes to print, it has been reported that two of the York people chosen to carry the Olympic torch as it passes through York in June 2012 are Stan Wild, Olympic gymnast, and Clive Warley, table tennis player, whose stories appear in this book.

BIBLIOGRAPHY

Buchanan, Ian. *Who's Who of UK and Great Britain: International Athletes 1896–1939*. National Union of Track Statisticians 2000

Daniels, Stephanie & Tedder, Anita. *A Proper Spectacle : Women Olympians 1900–1936*. ZeNaNa Press 2000

Hampton, Janie. *The Austerity Olympics* (1948). Aurum 2008

Illingworth, E. *Northern Counties Athletic Association 1879-1979*. NCAA Centenary Committee 1979

Murray, Hugh. *Opportunity of Leisure : The History of the York Railway Institute 1889–1989*. York Railway Institute 1989

Radnedge, Keir. *Olympic and World Records 2012*. Carlton 2011

York Civic Week Committee. *York Civic and Gala Week June 1934*. Herald Printing Works 1934

Kelly's and White's Street Directories of York

Yorkshire Evening Press (now York Press)

Yorkshire Gazette

FILM OF ATHLETES

www.britishpathe.com/video/gymnastics-championship - Stan Wild wins competition at England gymnastics championships 1969.

www.britishpathe.com - Walter Wilkinson wins 1 mile in British Games 1968 at White City. Walter Wilkinson second at AAA Championships 1968.

www.britishpathe.com - Anita Lonsbrough wins Anglo-Dutch swimming competition 1959, and 1960 Rome Olympics.

www.youtube.com

Interviews/footage of Richard Buck, Alf Patrick, Tom Ransley, Alan Rayment, Les Richards, John Sherwood

PUBLICATIONS BY THE SAME AUTHOR

The History of a Community : Fulford Road District of York.
University College of Ripon and York St John, 1984. Reprinted 1985

Alexina : A Woman in Wartime York. Voyager Publications, 1995

Rich in all but Money : Life in Hungate 1900-1938. York Archaeological Trust, 1996.
(Revised edition 2007)

Beyond the Postern Gate : A History of Fishergate and Fulford Road.
York Archaeological Trust, 1996

Humour, Heartache and Hope : Life in Walmgate.
York Archaeological Trust, 1996

York Voices. Tempus Publishing, 1999

Number 26 : The History of 26 St Saviourgate. Voyager Publications, 1999

Voices of St Paul's: An Oral History of St Paul's Church. (Edited)
William Sessions, 2001

Rhythm and Romance : An Oral History of Popular Music in York. Volume 1 : The Dance Band Years. York Oral History Society, 2002

Something in the Air : An Oral History of Popular Music in York. Volume 2 : The Beat Goes On. York Oral History Society, 2002

Rhythm and Romance : CD of The York Dance Band Era.
York Oral History Society, 2003

The Walmgate Story. Voyager Publications, 2006. Reprinted 2009

Something in the Air : CD of York Music in 1960s.
York Oral History Society, 2006

Rations, Raids and Romance : York in the Second World War.
York Archaeological Trust, 2008

Stonegate Voices. York Archaeological Trust, 2009.

The Story of Terry's. York Oral History Society, 2009

The Best Years of Our Lives : Secondary Education in York 1900-1985.
York Archaeological Trust, 2010

The Changing Face of Clifton. York Archaeological Trust, 2011